You and I

Ben Sadler You and I

(H) CONTEMPORARY ARTIST SERIES

Foreword

There is a great deal of pleasure to be had in looking at the paintings of Ben Sadler. This publication, the latest in the Hurtwood Contemporary Artist Series, focuses on two of Sadler's recent bodies of work: *Exclamations!*, 2023, and *You and I*, 2024, which both depict compelling portraits of people who don't exist.

Sadler is an ingenious artist who finds inspiration in a myriad of interests, from comic books, music videos and photographic archives to the mundane minutiae of everyday life. Born in 1977 in Birmingham, Sadler graduated in 1998 with a degree in Fine Art from the Ruskin School of Drawing and Fine Art at the University of Oxford, later completing a Masters in Sculpture at the Royal College of Art. His approach to art-making is broad – poetry, drawings, performances and public art sculptures – often with his collaborator, Phil Duckworth, as part of the successful art duo Juneau Projects.

So it is a delight to spend time studying Sadler's exquisite paintings and delve deeper into the line-up of imaginary characters and all the possibilities they bring with them. All are unique. Most meet our gaze, others are lost in contemplation, their eyes averted. They are uniformly elegant and curious, with a sense of timelessness and mystery. The (at times) muted colour palette, quirky fashions and pronounced brushstrokes evoke a powerful feeling of nostalgia. But what, if anything, connects the figures in the series *You and I*? The answer is simple: they are all visitors to art exhibitions. As Sadler explains, the paintings 'led me to think about art openings and the very specific feelings I have at these events'.

Looking at art can be tricky – even veteran art enthusiasts might nervously navigate exhibitions that feel utterly unrelatable while observing others who are confidently engrossed. I recall my young son accompanying me to a show and in his frustration whining, 'Just tell me what I should feel!' The ambivalence is evident in the faces of Sadler's gallery-goers, their bemused expressions and bored silences meeting our gaze. People love watching people – it can be the basis for our projections and self-reflections – and here with their teasing, ambiguous titles, from A to Z (or thereabouts), there is joy and wit in abundance. It is less to do with capturing the real than stirring a desire to invent a narrative to put upon an image, to imagine a personality. In her text, Catherine O'Flynn offers wonderful characterisations, like surreal exhibition labels, leading our imaginations further. The interview between Sadler and Ceri Hand offers a rich insight into the life of the artist and the experiences that influence his work.

As John Berger states in *Ways of Looking*, 'Behind every glance is judgement.' Perhaps that has something to do with the anxiety of observing art: we feel part of the scrutiny, voyeurism and the performance. Yet here among Sadler's cast, we can also share in the glorious camaraderie of experiencing art together, forever watching, you and I.

Deborah Kermode
CEO and Artistic Director, MAC, Birmingham

The Imaginary Lives of Imaginary People by Catherine O'Flynn

I spent about four hours a day, every day watching television when I was a child. It wasn't time wasted. There are many situations and phenomena about which I learnt almost everything I know from watching TV. The list is long but would include: standard kidnap protocol; golf; phone tapping; double-sided Sellotape; marital infidelity; youth clubs; quicksand; exhibition openings.

I didn't grow up in a household that regularly attended art shows. I guess few did. We didn't attend the openings of exhibitions, or openings of new productions of Chekhov at the National, or openings of supermarkets with ribbons cut by zany local radio presenters. Openings in general did not figure in our lives.

My first awareness of the art world came from American, specifically LA-based, television series of the 1970s. The kinds of galleries shown in those television programmes were not like Birmingham Museum & Art Gallery – the only example I knew. They were airy white spaces showing almost exclusively contemporary art. Openings were shown to be convivial events – filled with exotic people wearing kooky floppy hats and long, slinky waistcoats, clinking champagne glasses – but also somewhat fraught and awkward. Our hapless protagonists were often portrayed as sceptical of the art on display, failing to understand or appreciate it in some way, or saying or doing the wrong thing. The other attendees would be supercilious, or pretentious, or somewhat unhinged.

It was entirely alien to me except in one respect. The slow shuffling procession from one painting to another, pausing to contemplate and reflect, was something with which I had some familiarity. I'd done it for as long as I could remember each year in my parish church while participating in the Stations of the Cross. This involved moving around the gloomy interior of St Joseph's nave to stand and contemplate fourteen murky Victorian oil paintings of Jesus on the day of his crucifixion, while the priest led us in prayers. We weren't meant to be identifying or interrogating the artistic choices underlying each depiction, but rather reflecting on Christ's sacrifice. The titles engraved at the bottom of each frame were dogged in their toneless cataloguing: *Jesus falls the first time*; *Jesus falls the second time*; *Jesus falls the third time*; *Jesus is stripped of his garments*; *Jesus dies on the cross*. Together the stations formed a jerky, stop-motion horror film: the nails in the flesh; the spear in the side; the crown of thorns. The only relief from the cruelty and pain was to turn my eyes to the reassuring plaster statue of St Joseph holding a piece of wood. I liked to think of him busy in his carpentry workshop on Good Friday, making a spice rack while the atrocities up on the hill passed him by. I had a bad feeling that like those LA cops/medical examiners/private investigators I wasn't responding to the images in the right way. There was some guilt attached to this, also potential damnation.

It's a feeling that still remains when I attend exhibitions or openings. I begin to question myself. Am I spending the right amount of time absorbing and considering each artwork or am I being too cursory? Am I engaging fully? Am I open to everything? Am I finding any common ground between my experience of existence and the artist's? Am I supposed to? Am I thinking of anything other than myself and my responses? Am I the exhibit?

The focus on looking and seeing can make doing so feel performative and self-conscious. I am acting the role of a gallery attendee while also being a gallery attendee. I look at the other people staring fixedly at the art works and I try and imagine what thoughts they are having as perhaps they are imagining mine. I try and imagine the kinds of lives they live as perhaps they are imagining mine. I imagine myself as one of those people and gradually we all become imaginary.

*

Apple – looks more intelligent than they are and this is both a good and a bad thing. Relationships start well but end badly. They try to project their genuine goofiness but never quite carry it off. They want to shout and tell the world: 'There's nothing much going on in here.'

Bat – has moved up in the world. She has six bedrooms, five bathrooms and 107 scented candles. She keeps telling her kids how lucky they are to have a bathroom each. She wonders now, did she leave food out for them? Did she put the matches away?

Cat – only pretends to look at the paintings. He has other things on his mind. Chief among them is the worry that she will show up with her grisly relatives. The muscles in his neck are tense. Nowhere is safe anymore. His peace of mind gone forever.

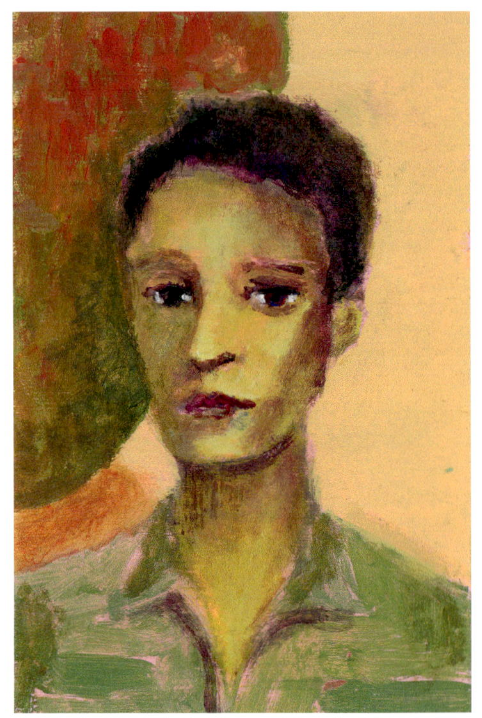

Dinosaur – wonders how long it will be before someone mentions the resemblance. If it bothered him that much he could change his hairstyle but why should he? He waits for someone to say it, but nobody does. Playing it cool, he thinks. Typical of this crowd.

Elephant – can't believe that they've changed the recipe of his favourite black cherry jam. It was one simple, uncomplicated good thing in his life and now they've fucked it up with extra fruit. It was fine as it was! Now it all begins again.

Flowers – worries about aging. He doesn't know how to be an older person and all the advice seems to focus on the wrong things. He wants a straightforward, step-by-step guide on how to get through each day from the moment he wakes to the moment he dips back into the blackness.

Guitar – is not liked by her pupils. Her temper is frightening and she says mean things loud enough to be heard. The children think she has death-ray vision and only a particular type of rollerball from Poundland can protect them from this. Also, if they look directly at her feet they will die.

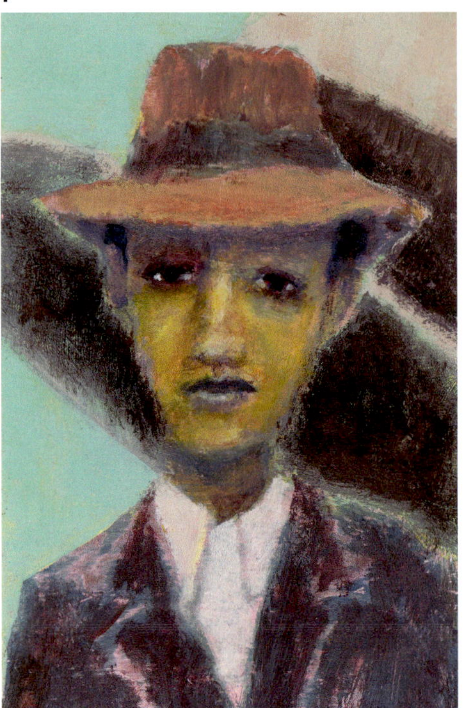

Hat – is now wondering if the hat was a mistake. In the pale expanse of the gallery it feels a much larger statement than it had in his bedroom, much larger than he intended. The others look at him and they see only the hat. He is defined by it, imprisoned by it.

Jaguar – was the drummer in a short-lived, chart-topping all-girl act in the eighties. They toured the world and remain popular in Turkey due to their big hit 'Ankara, Ankara'. She was persuaded to appear in the video dressed as a mermaid and that's where, historically, a lot of the trouble started.

Kite – wonders what the others are thinking. Two paintings stand out for him, but he isn't able to say why; if he could he would like them less. He feels affable and exuberant. The kind of mood that makes you say, 'How do?' in a northern accent to strangers and then regret it instantly.

Lines – was good at drawing at primary school. She got a crazy amount of praise and popularity as a result. Now nobody gives a hoot about her art. It's a funny world. She wants to leave soon.

Masks – has heard the words 'Cheer up, it might never happen' on more occasions than she would care to remember. Occasions on which she has in fact been perfectly cheerful, joyous even. She has come to accept that her face is telling a story that is not her own. She wonders if there is someone out there who has her true face, transmitting equanimity while experiencing utter despair.

Night – didn't want to come. He's a stay-at-home kind of guy. He likes watching the cookery programmes and being the audience volunteer for his son's appalling magic tricks. He's enjoying it though. He decides to buy everything.

Orange – is a member of a late seventies/early eighties radical feminist theatre group. She puts honey instead of sugar in her tea. She won't wear tights, but is fine with pop socks. She enjoys Mellow Birds coffee but hides the fact from her friends. She is in an on-off relationship with an idiotic man called Felipe. She has painted her kitchen red.

Plants – has seen some preposterous hats already.

Quill – is always quiet at work. 'The quiet ones are the worst,' a colleague jokes, implying some hidden chaos or noise or mischief where there is none. She is quiet at work and at home, quiet inside and out, silenced daily by the sheer volume of things other people find to think and say.

Ribbon – is gambling again. He's moved the whole family to England to escape and now it has started up again. They're living in a terrible place called Birmingham and his wife neither respects nor loves him anymore. His sons are sullen, but his daughter is flourishing. Each day she shines brighter and lifts them all.

Spots – turns when he enters the room. She's forgotten how much she misses him. How has it been so long? He's the only one who remembers the ghost on the nineteenth floor and the business with the lifts. It's moments before she realises it isn't him.

Tree – lives in a tiny bedsit in Queens. She's written two unpublished novels. She never even sent them to publishers, they were just for her. She spends her days riding the subway. She's running low on funds but today's the day she meets Tony and her life will change.

Vase – is a historical side-note, glimpsed in early, barely recognisable photos of his daughter who went on to become famous all over the world. Throughout her brief life she was customarily referred to as a sex symbol and this makes him think of Greek letters, or hieroglyphs, stray fragments of mathematical notation. But when he remembers her, he thinks of cool, clean sand running through his fingers.

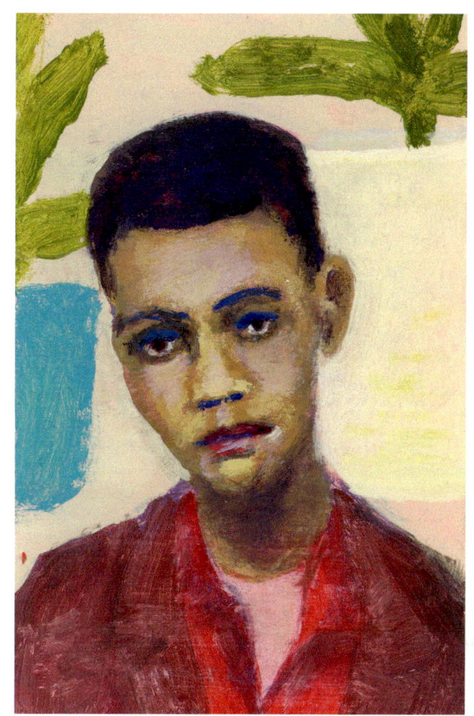

3

1 *Apple*, 2024
2 *Hat*, 2024
3 *Plants*, 2024

Watermelon – was a lesser-known bank robber during the great depression. He never got rich, but he survived and evaded capture. After the war he went straight and set up a chain of dry-cleaners in the Bay area. Buying art is his great indulgence.

Xylophone – is a good listener, but even he has his limits. He feels as if most of his life has been passed listening to this bloke go on and on. He's forgotten how it started, lost track of what he's saying. Words lose their meaning, language breaks down, the room tilts and his breath won't come. The last thing he sees is an apple.

Yacht – was engaged twice before she married Dermot. She still thinks about Michael. He had a much sweeter temperament and a generous nature. A lovely smile too. He couldn't drive though so that was the end of that.

Zebra – if she can work something to her own advantage she will. She is a lifelong queue-jumper and petty thief. She has a great career in product design but never contributes to leaving collections. The only thing in this world that she cares about is her bloody terrapins.

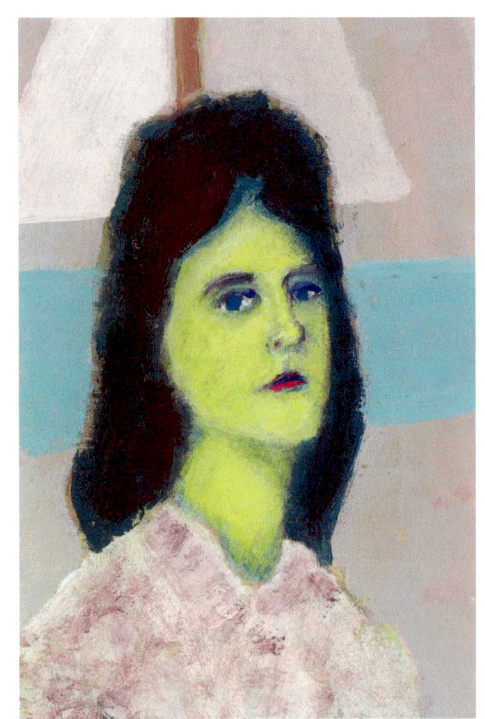

4

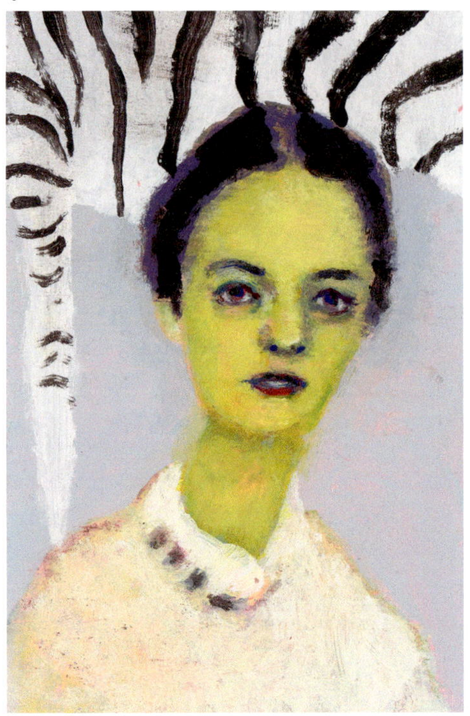

5

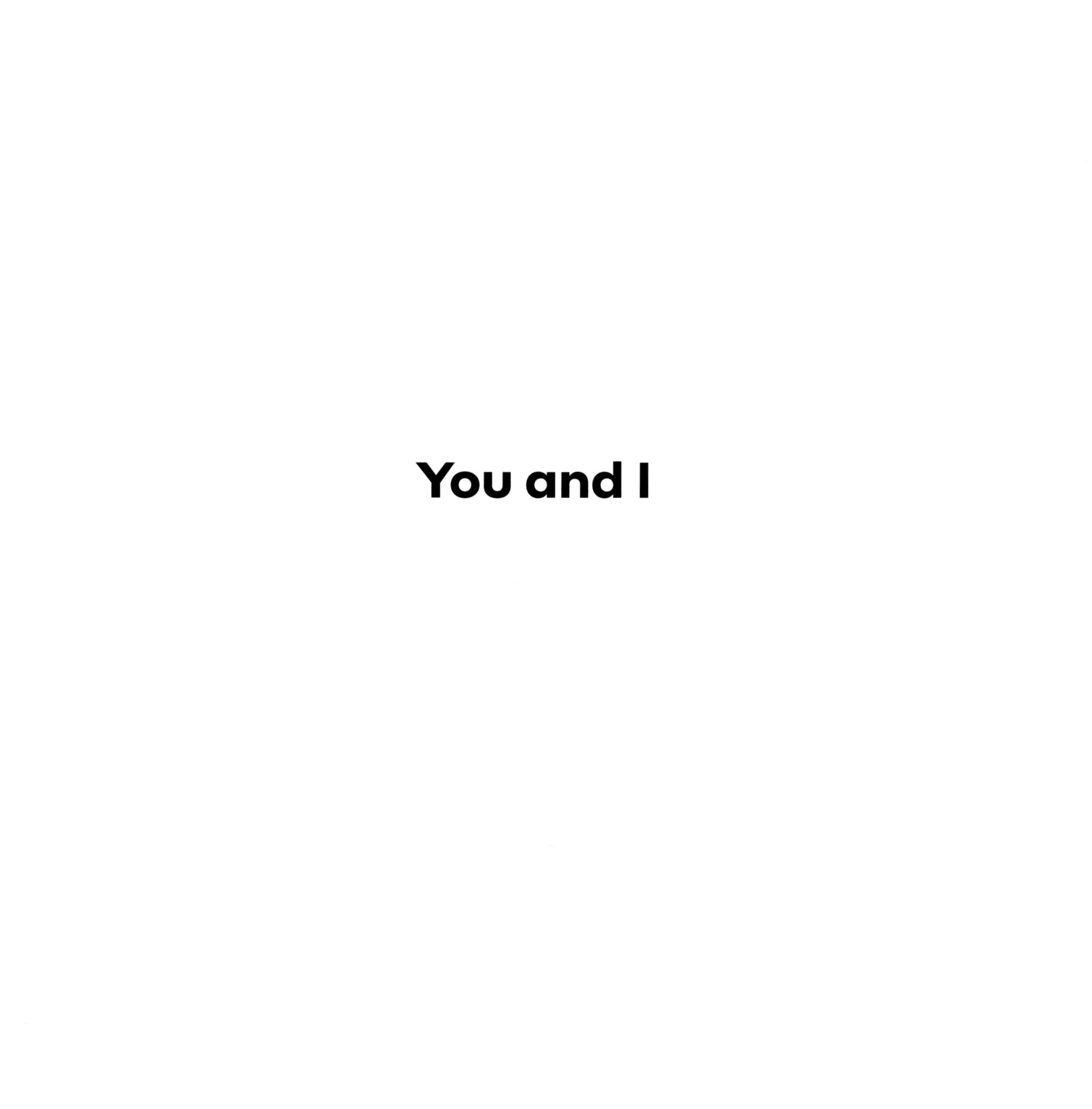

You and I

Apple, 2024
All works acrylic on board, 15.3 x 9.3 cm (6 x 3¾ in.)

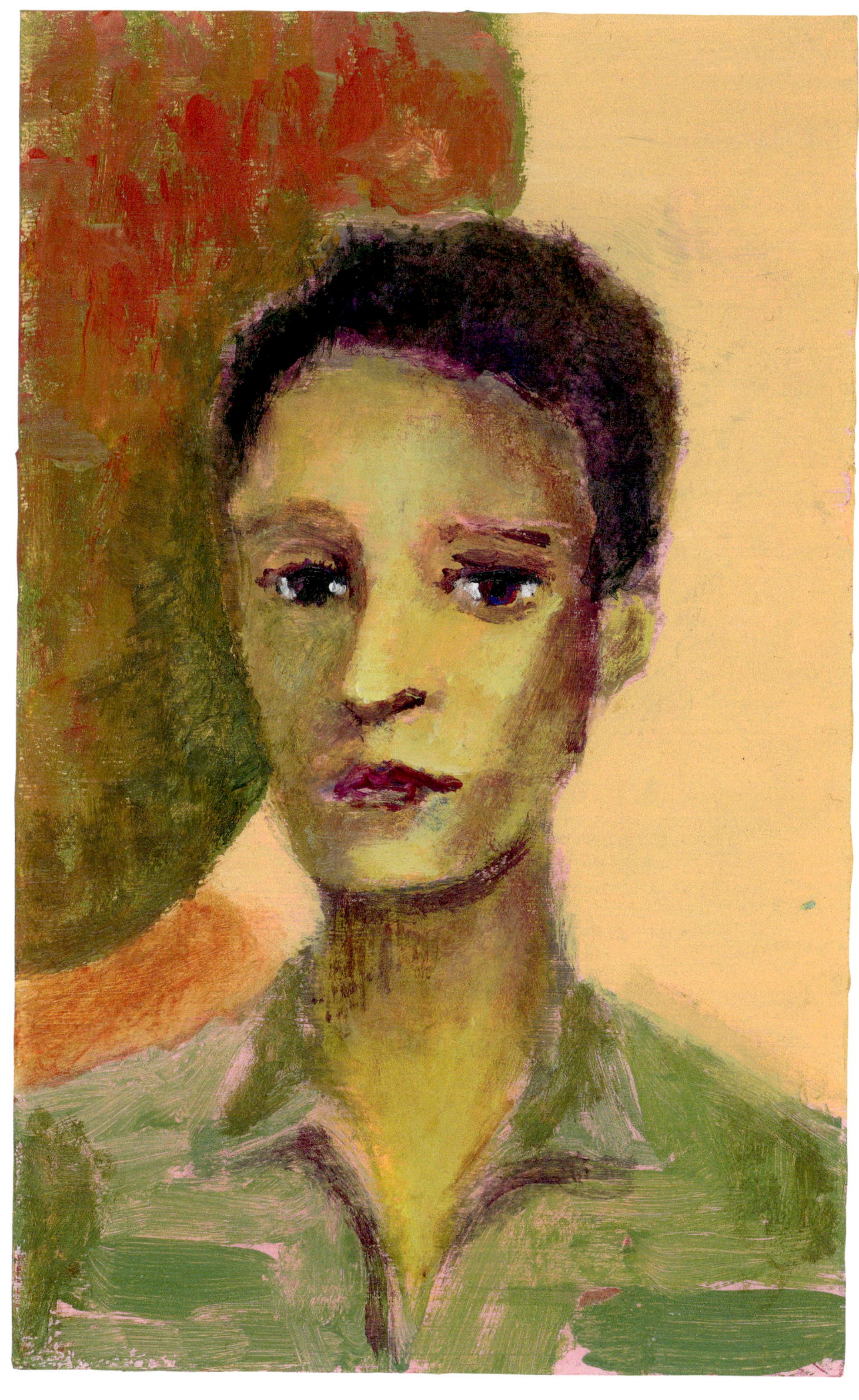

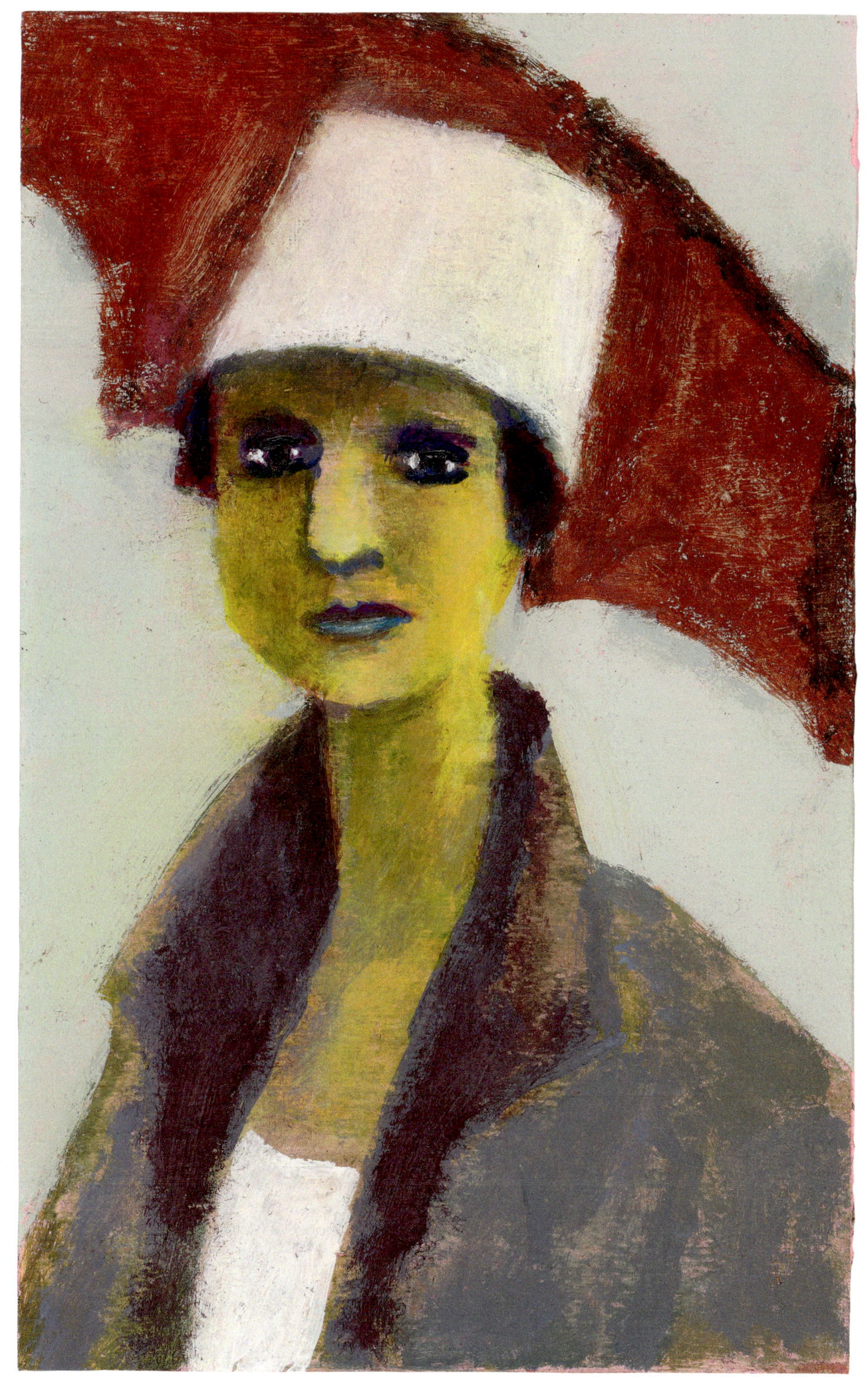

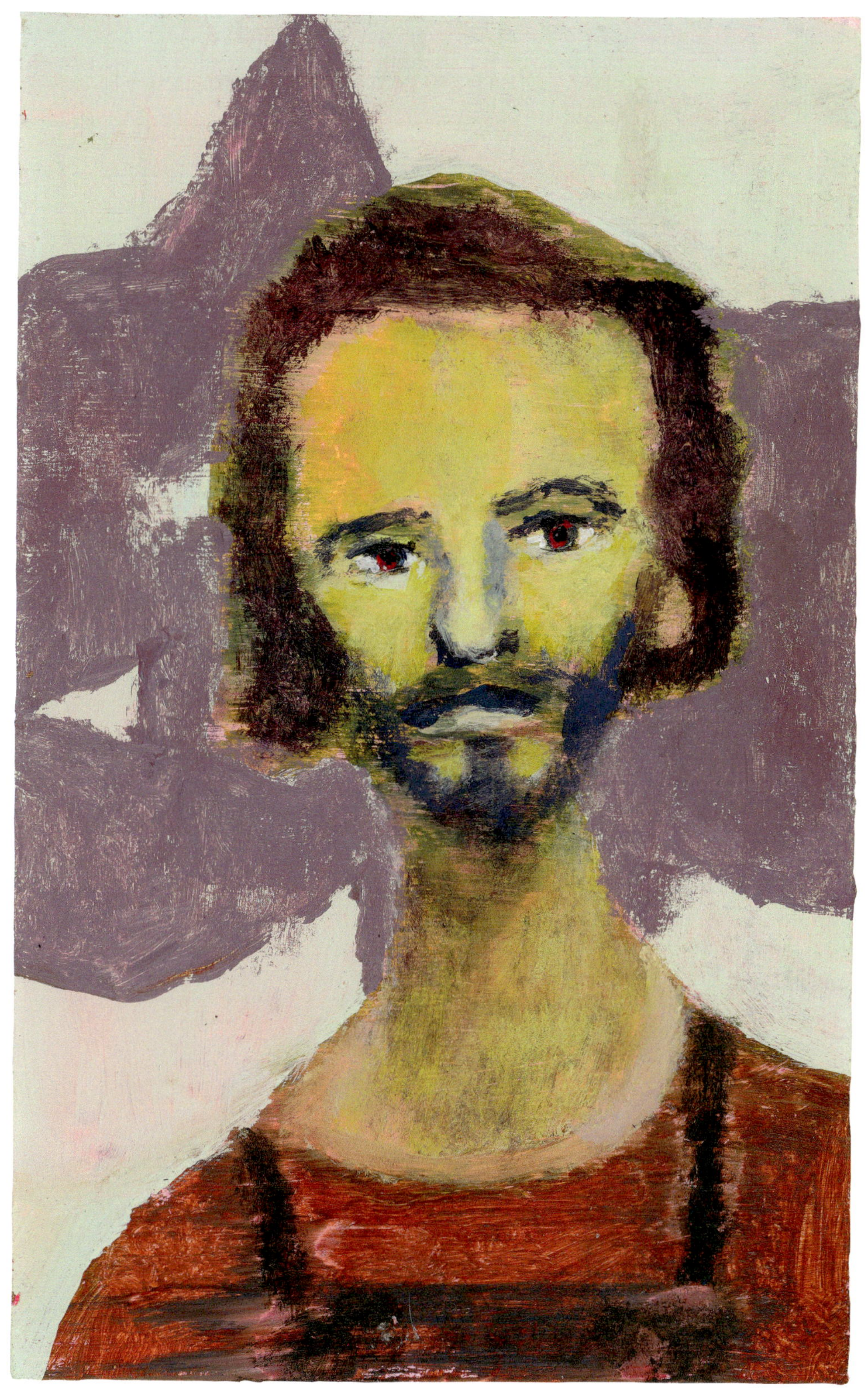

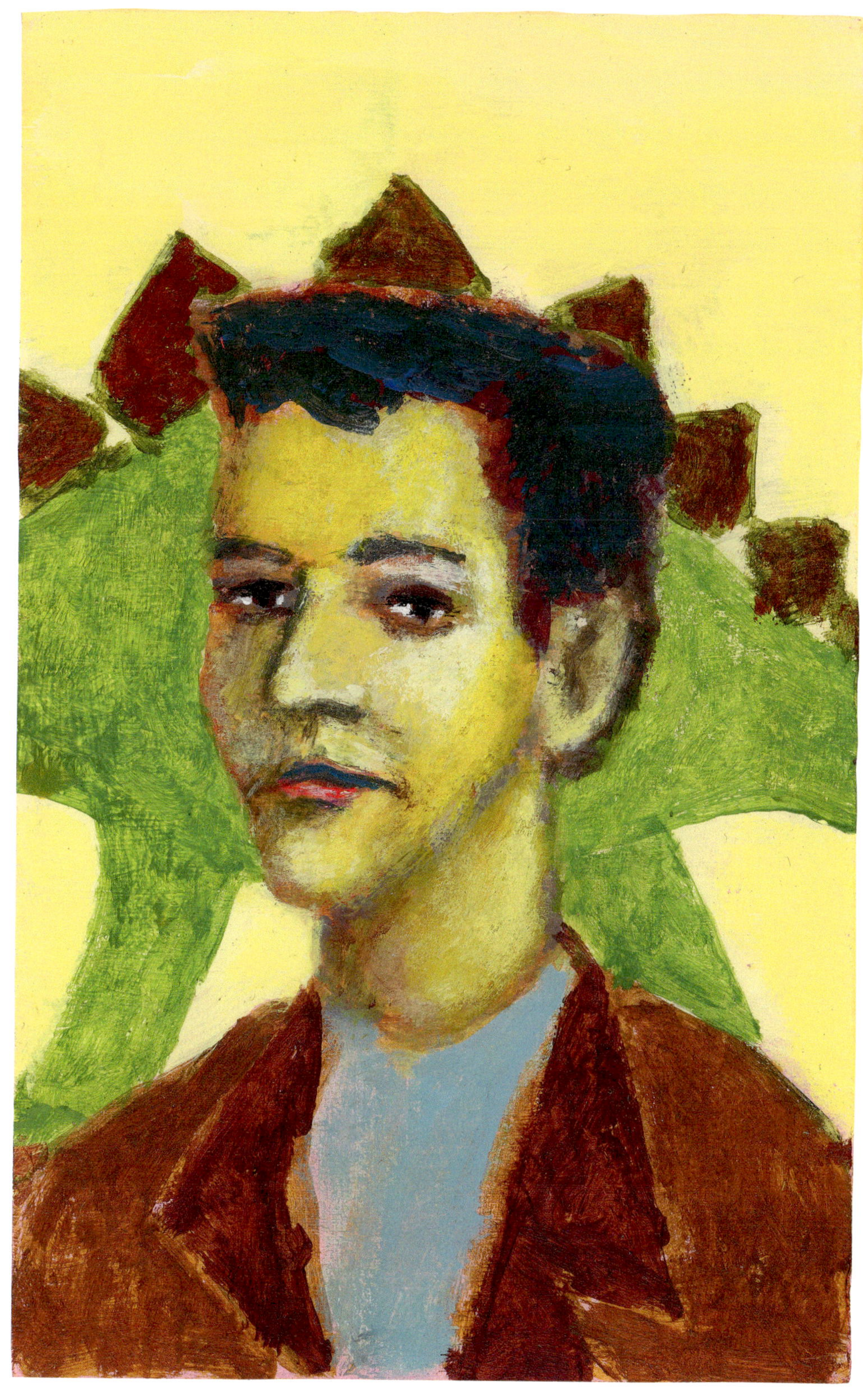

Elephant, 2024

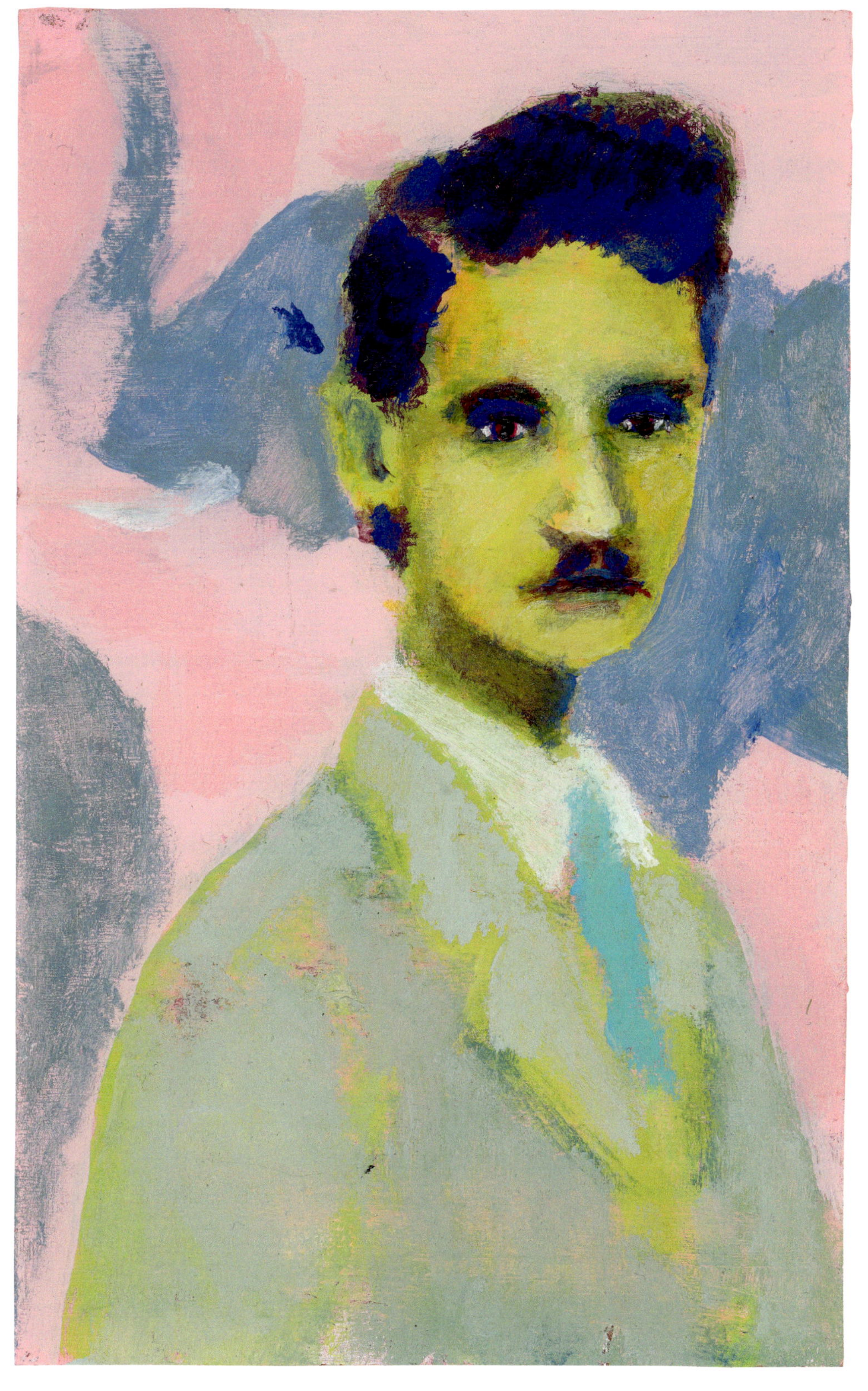

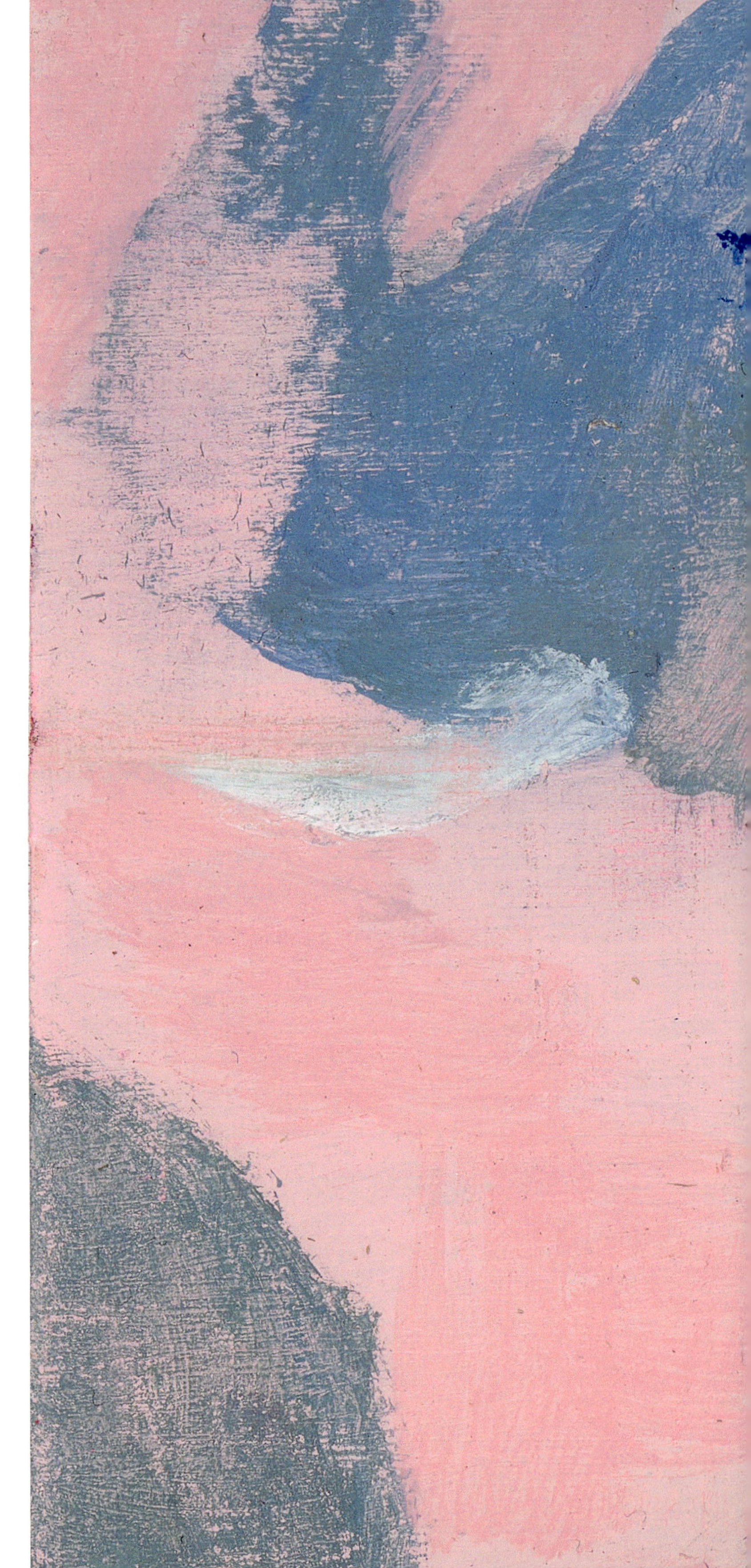

Elephant, 2024 (detail)

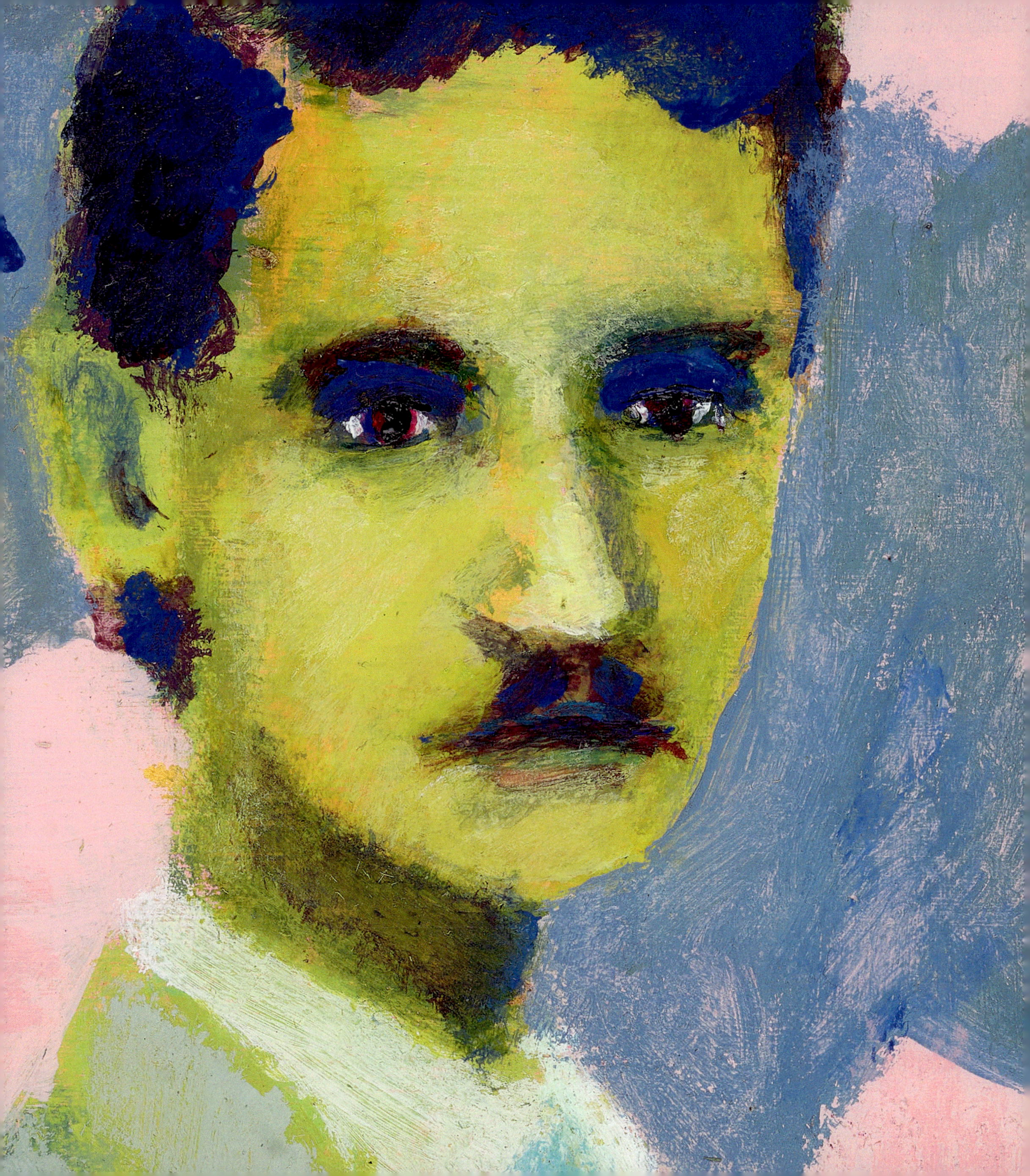

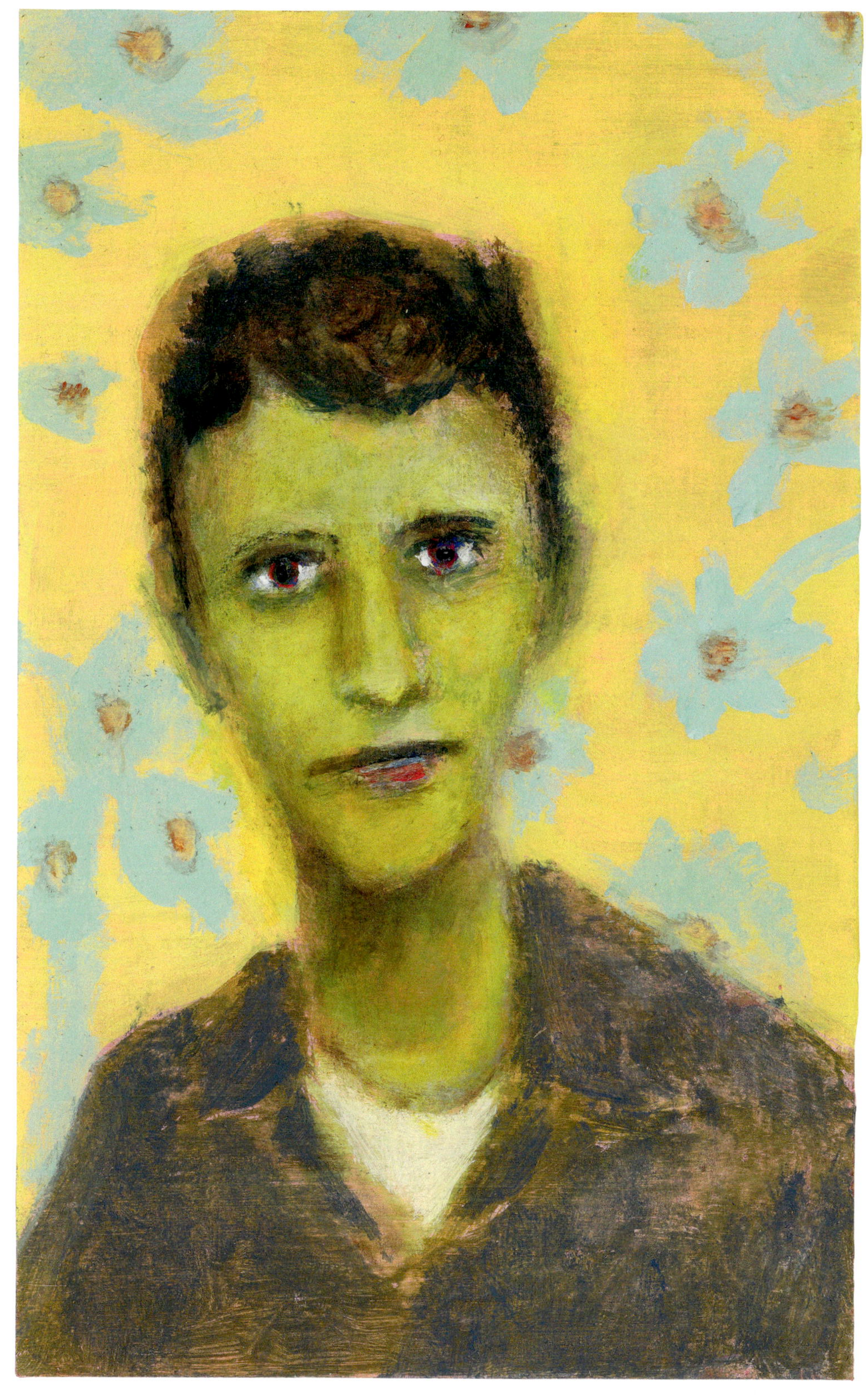

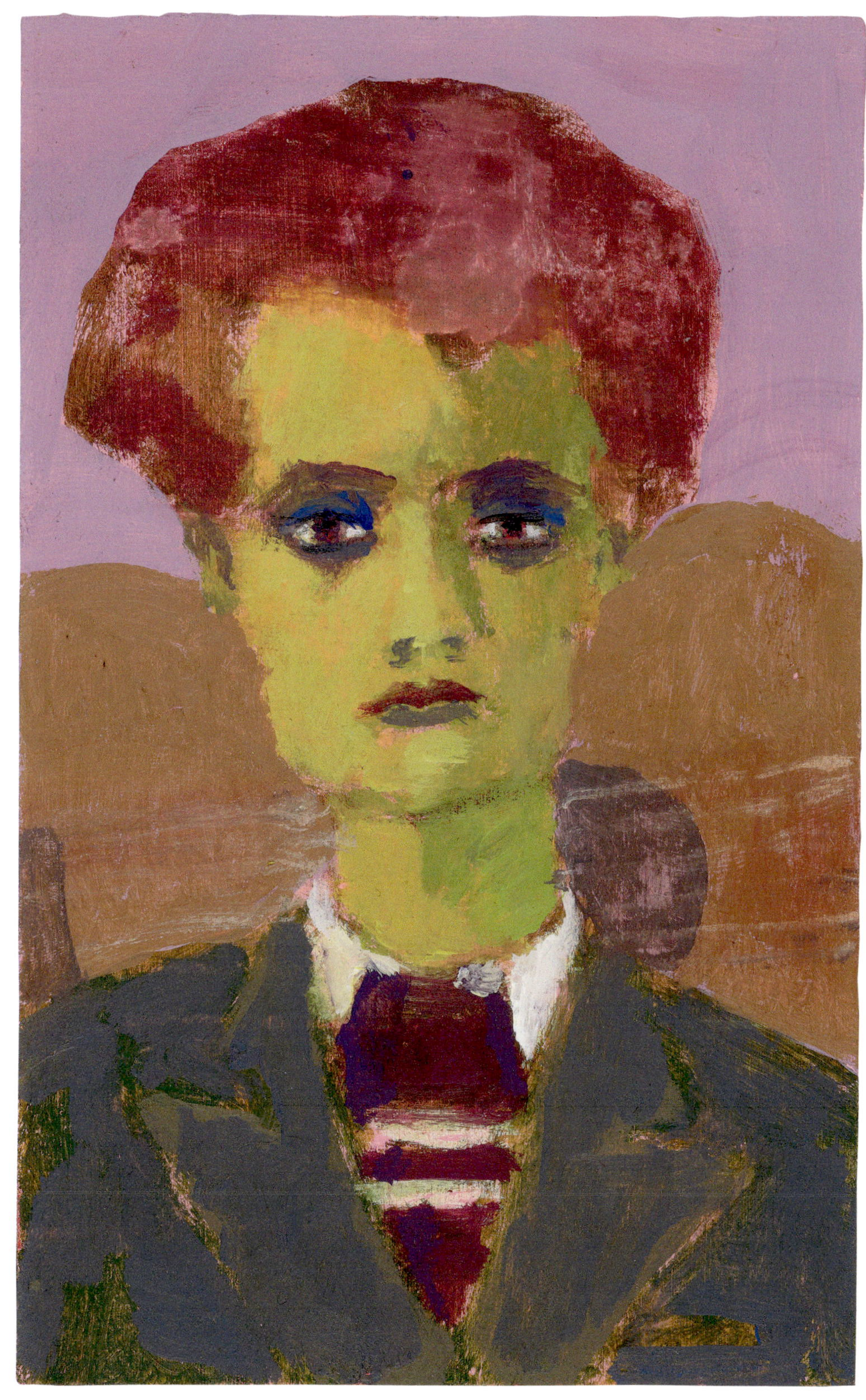

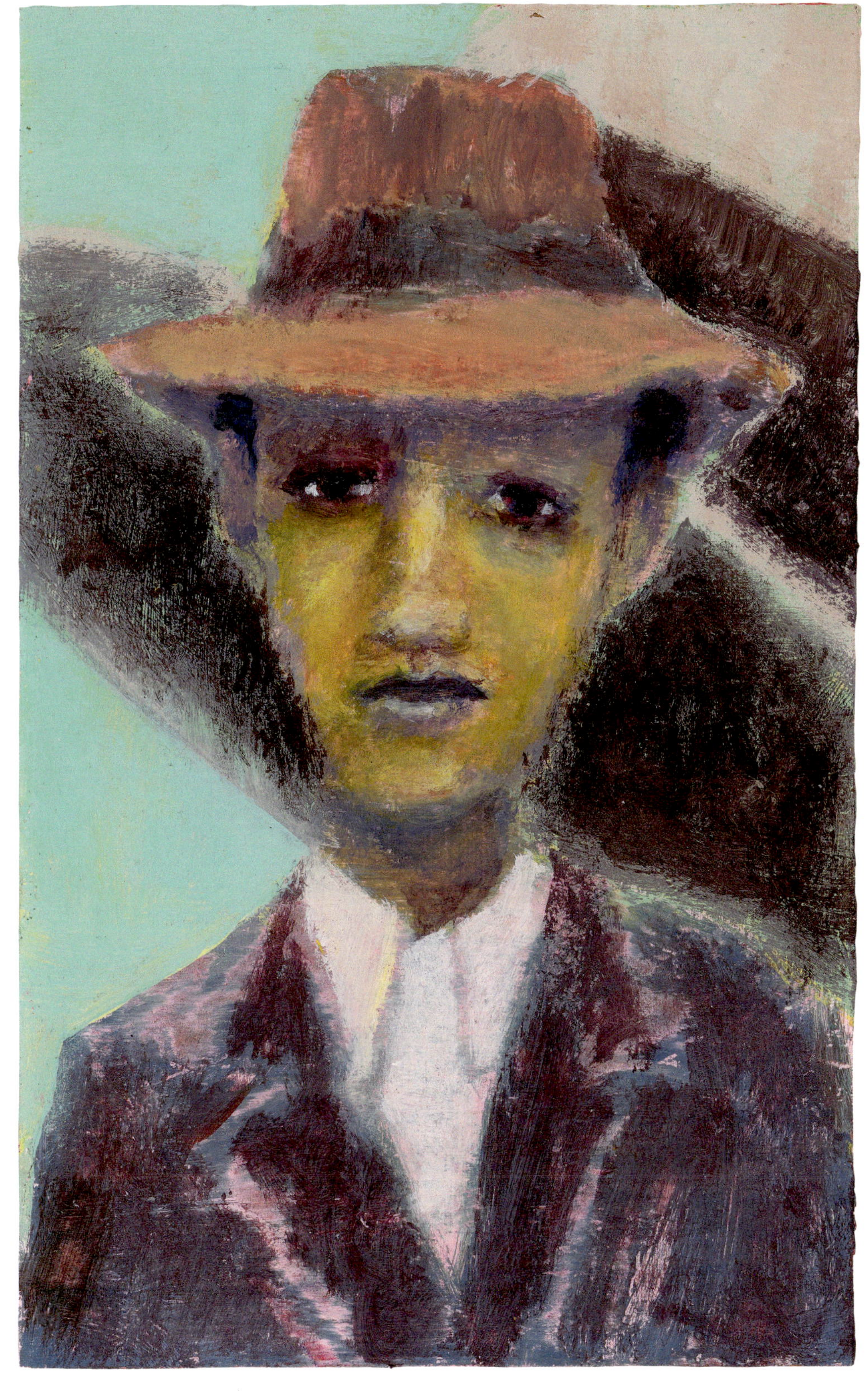

Hat, 2024 (detail)

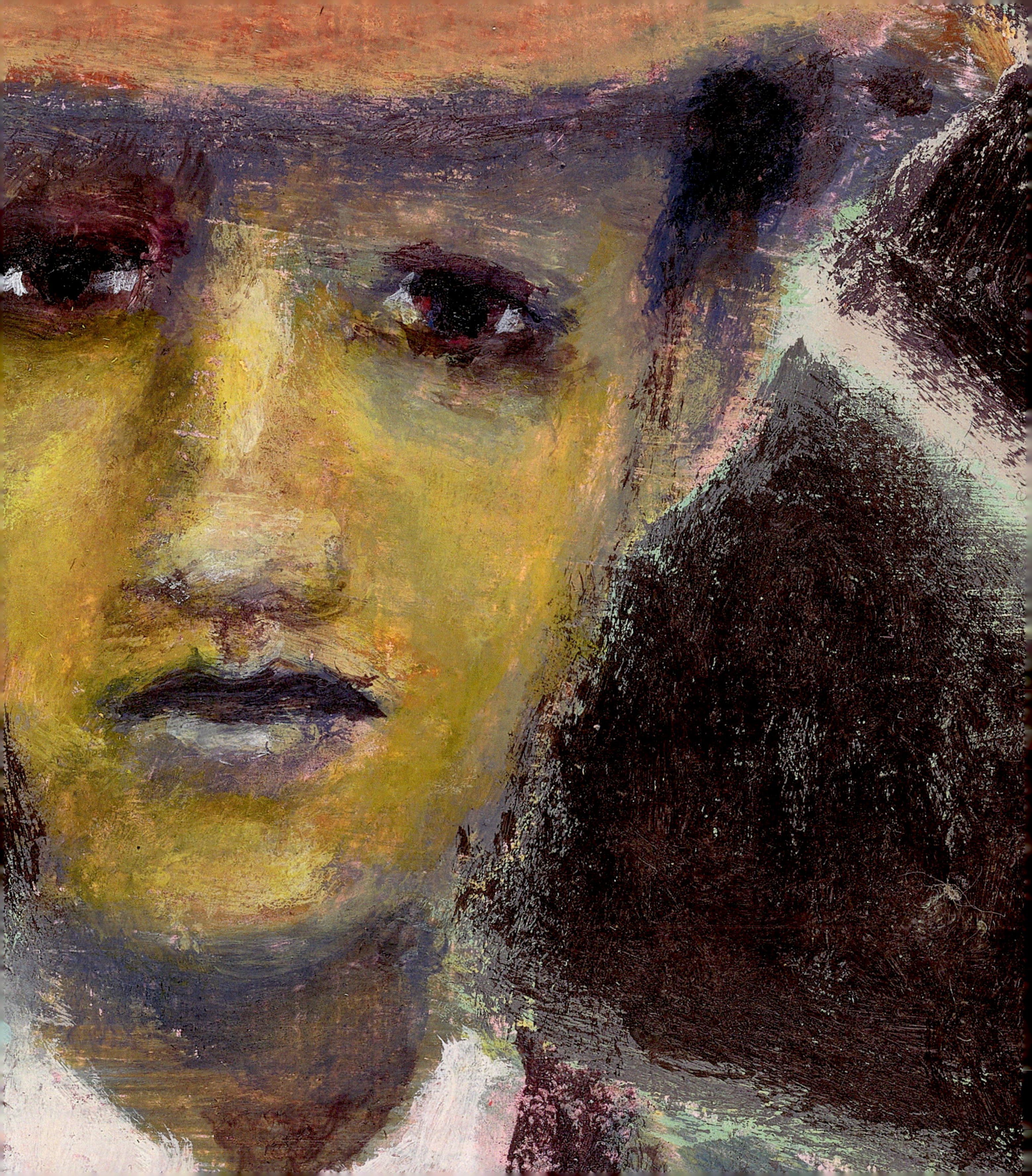

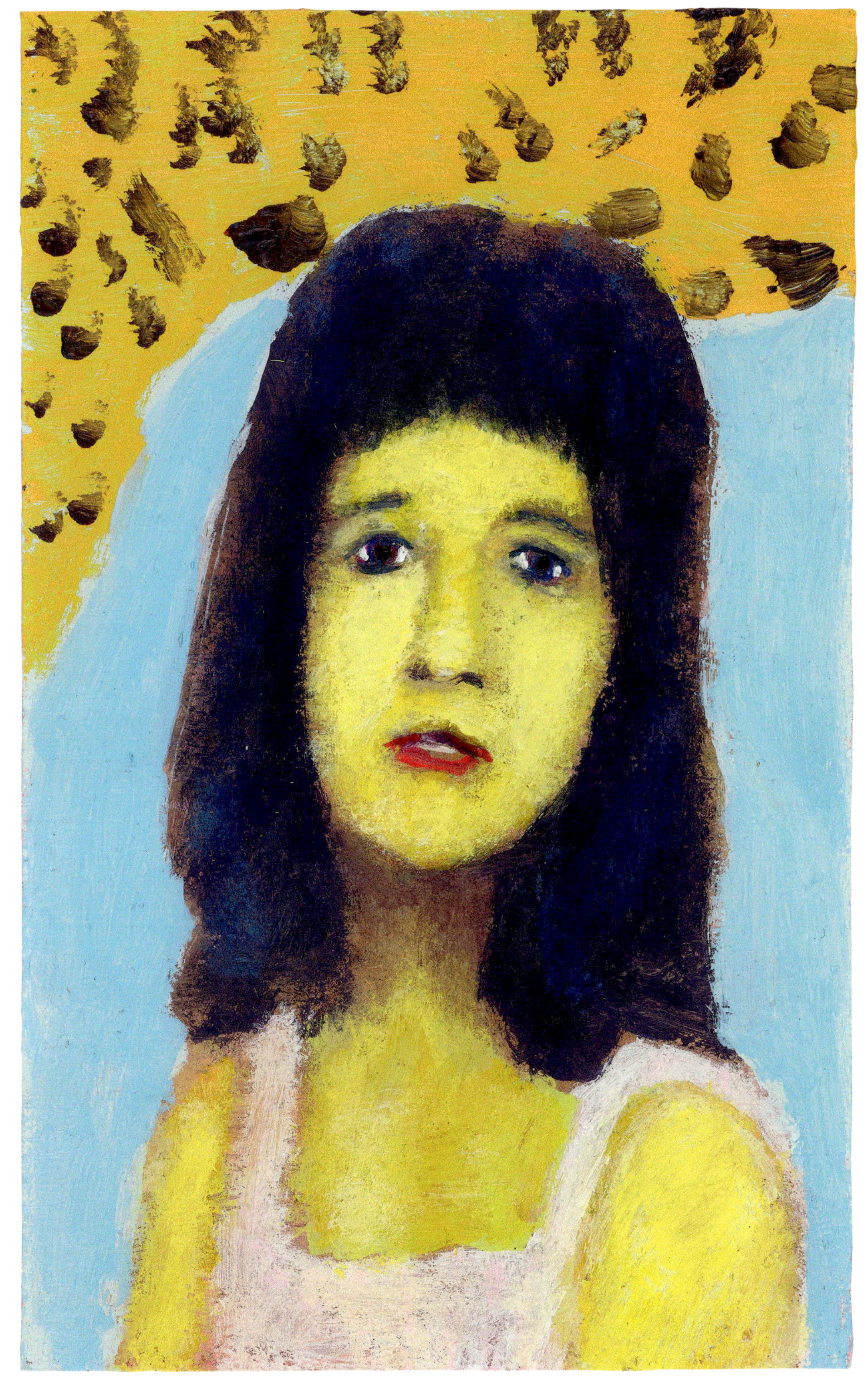

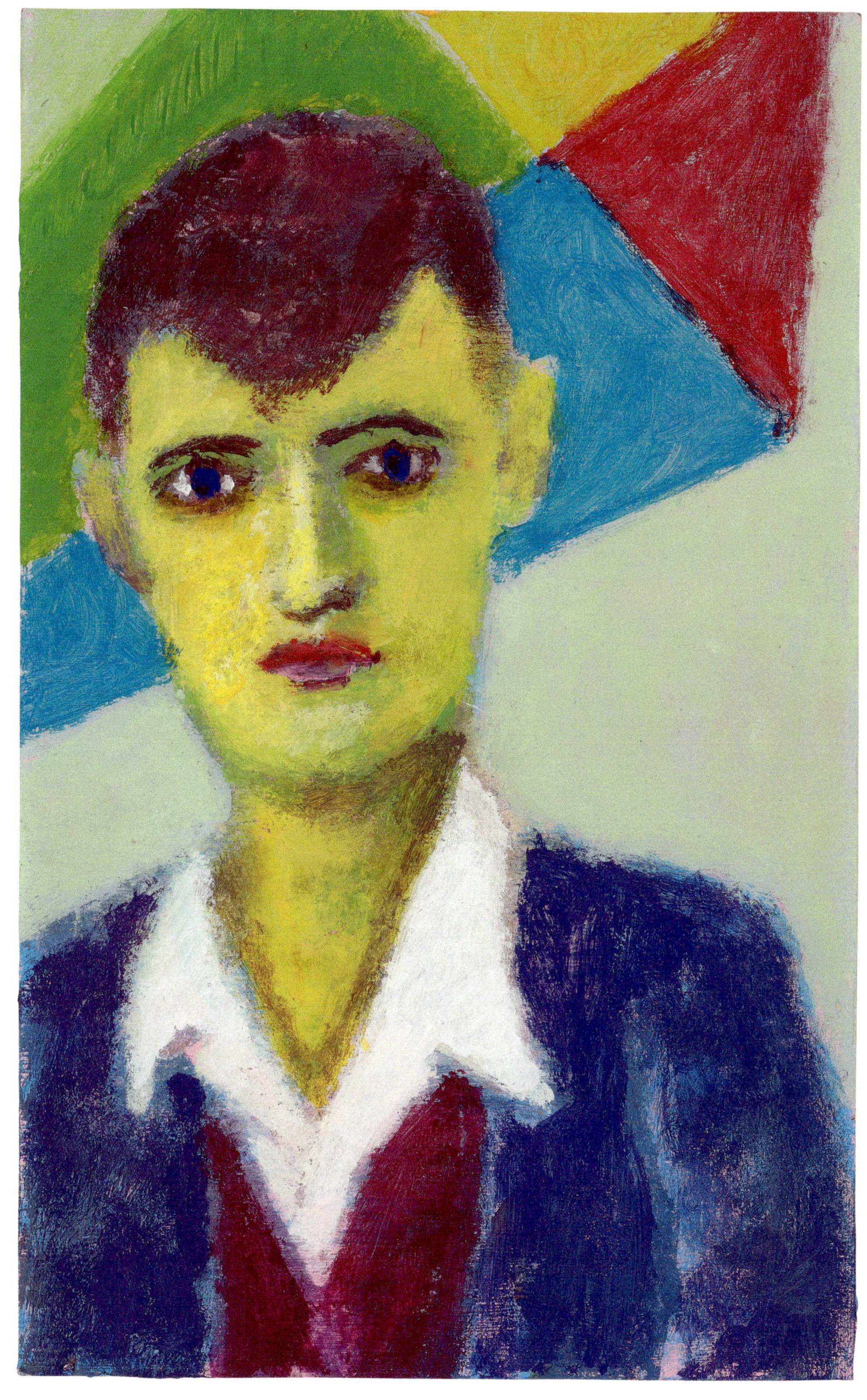

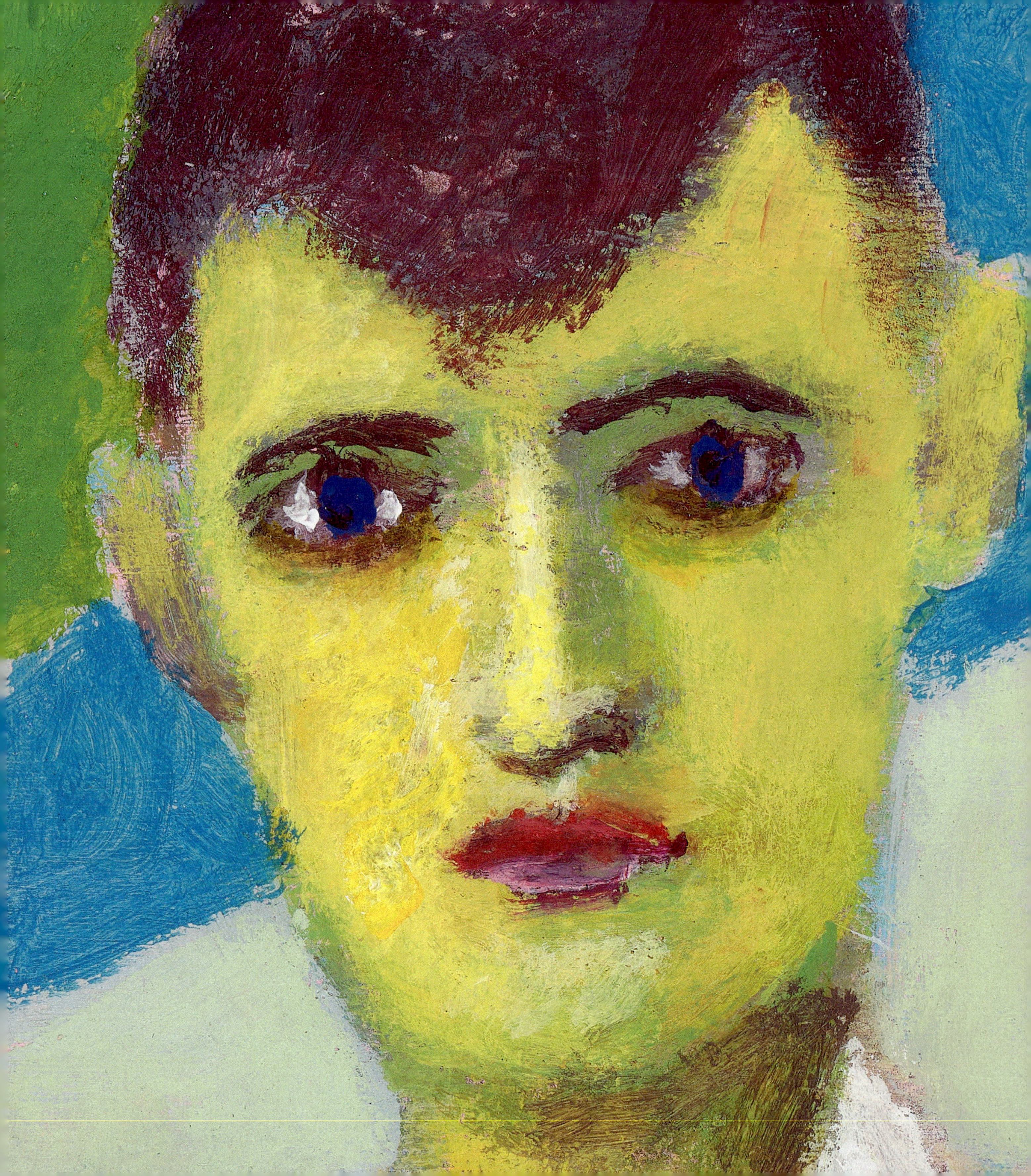

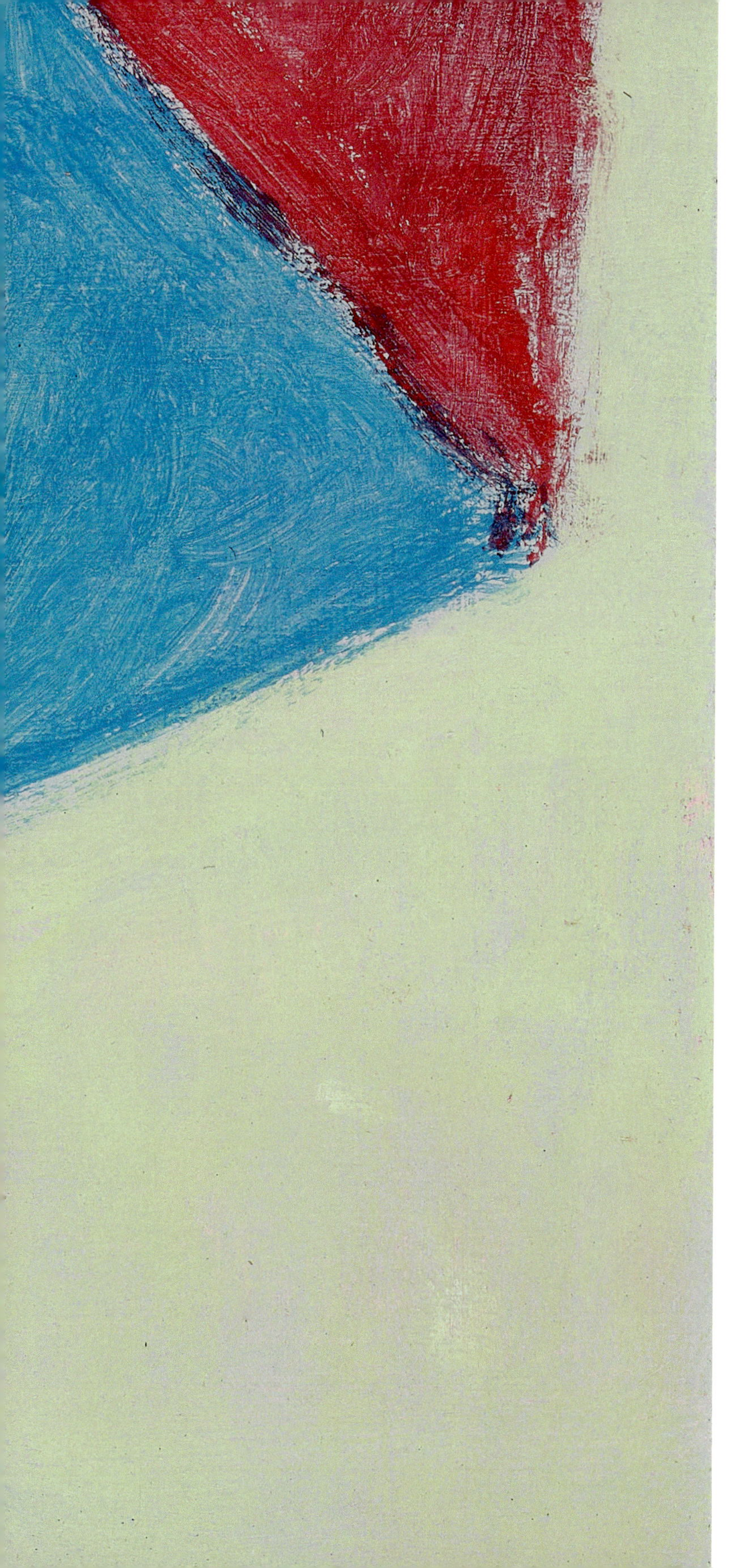

Kite, 2024 (detail)

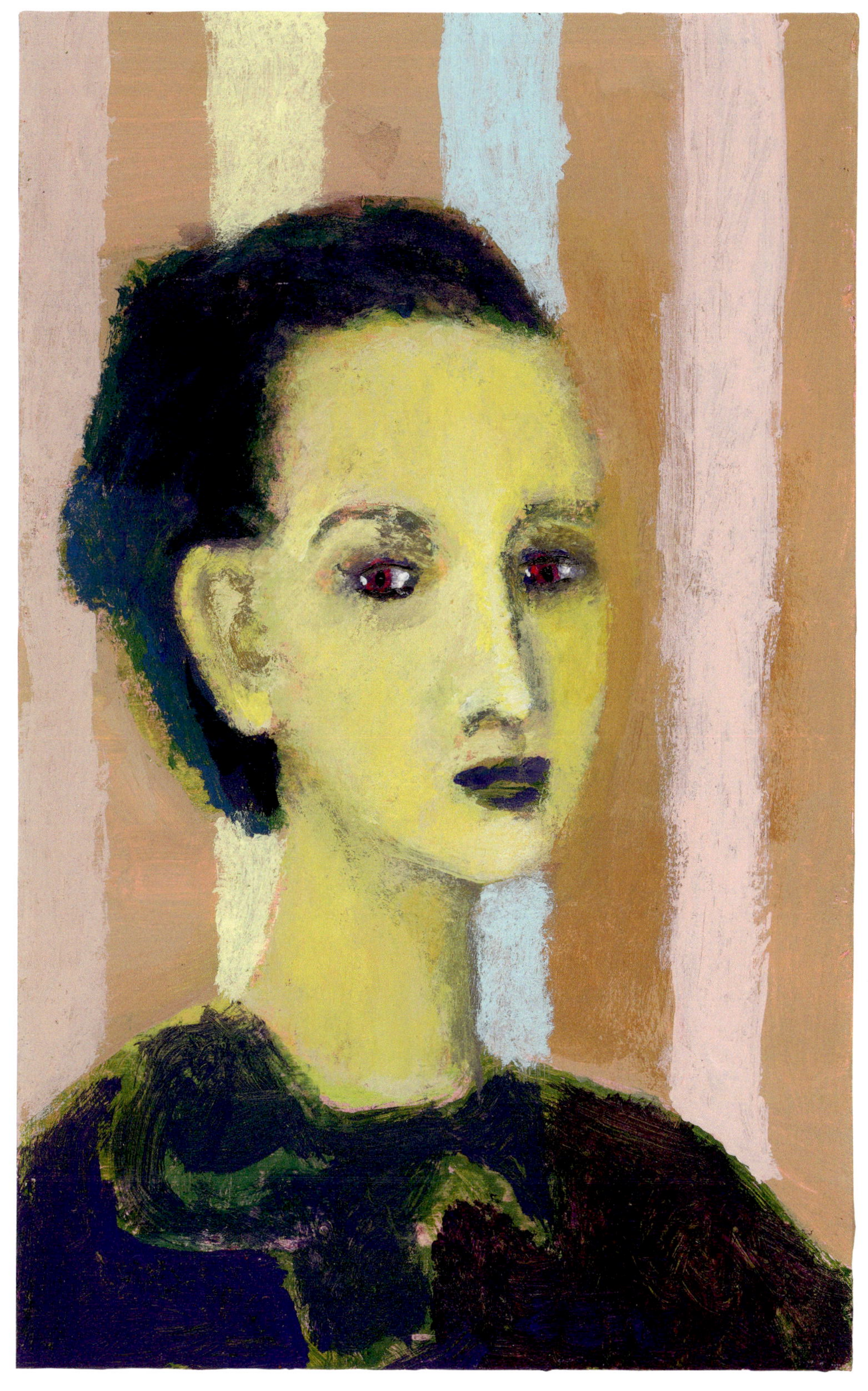

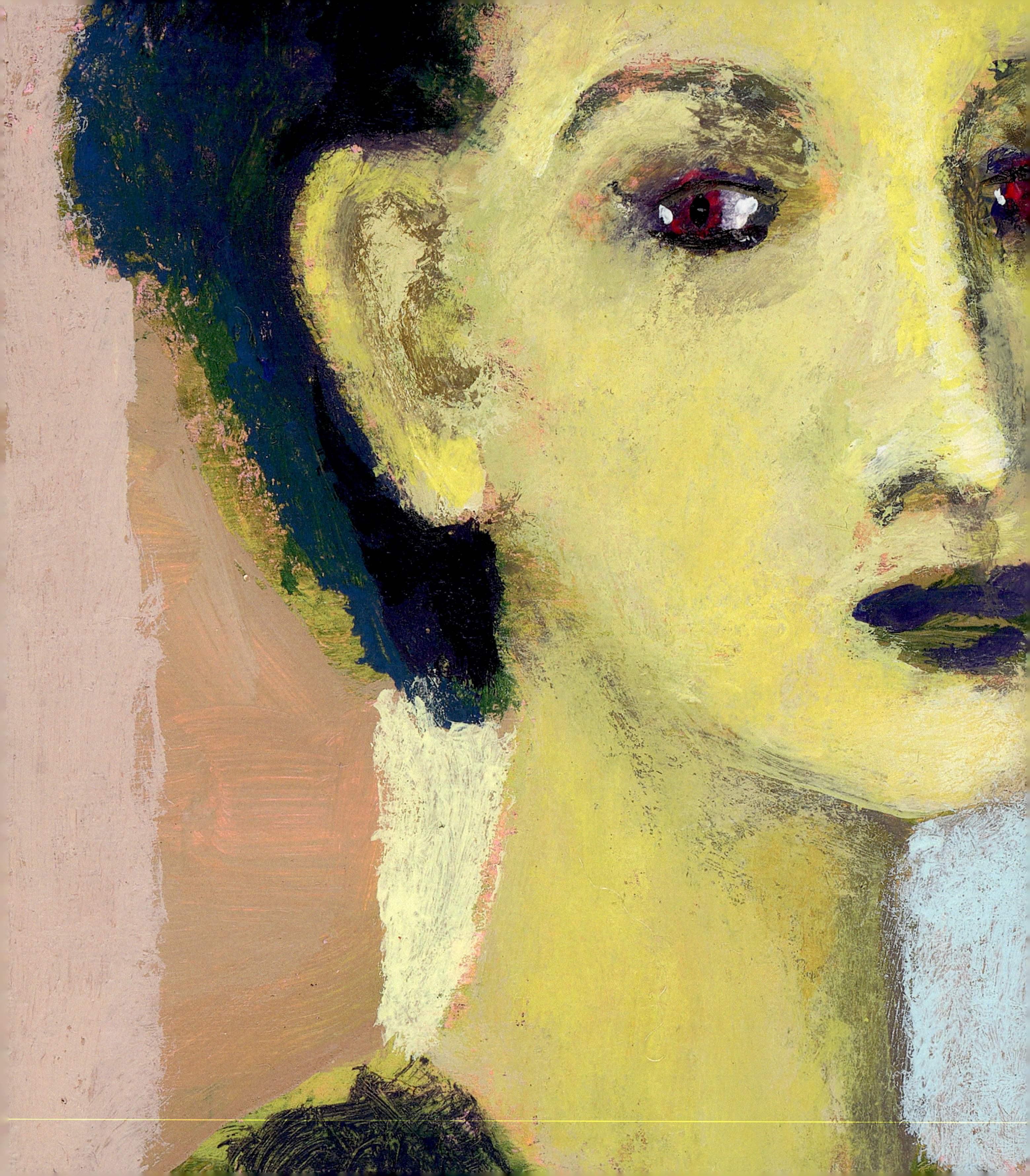

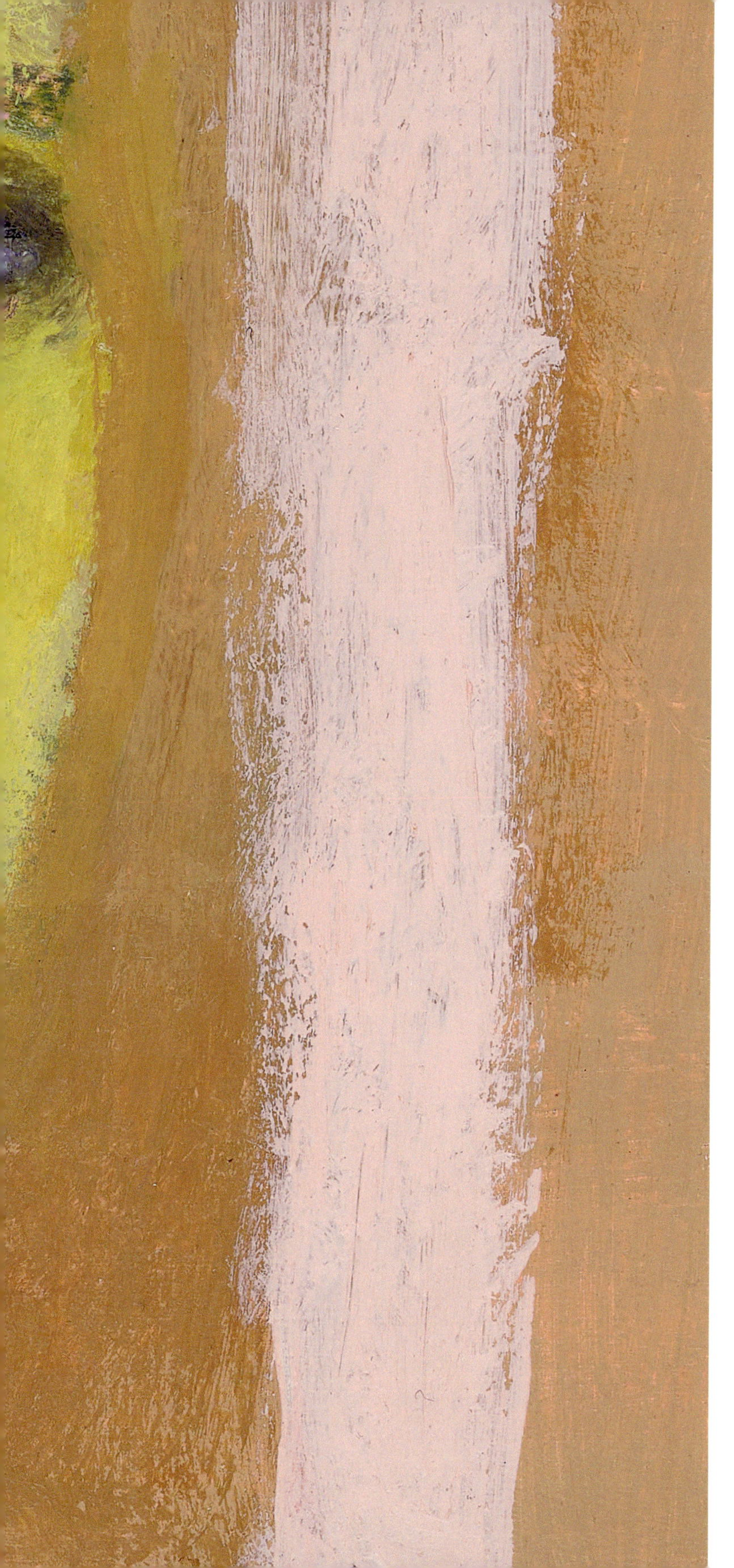

Lines, 2024 (detail)

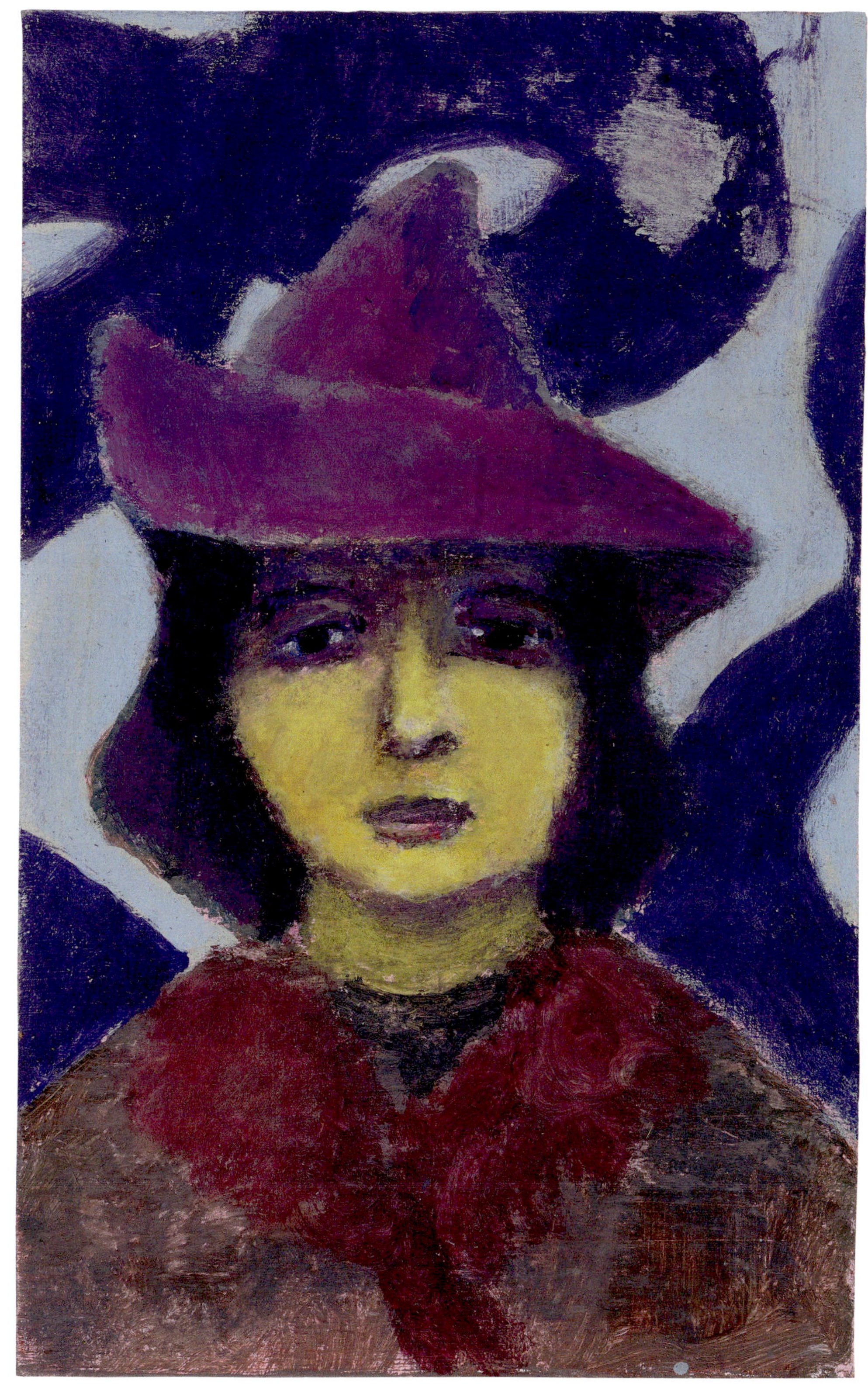

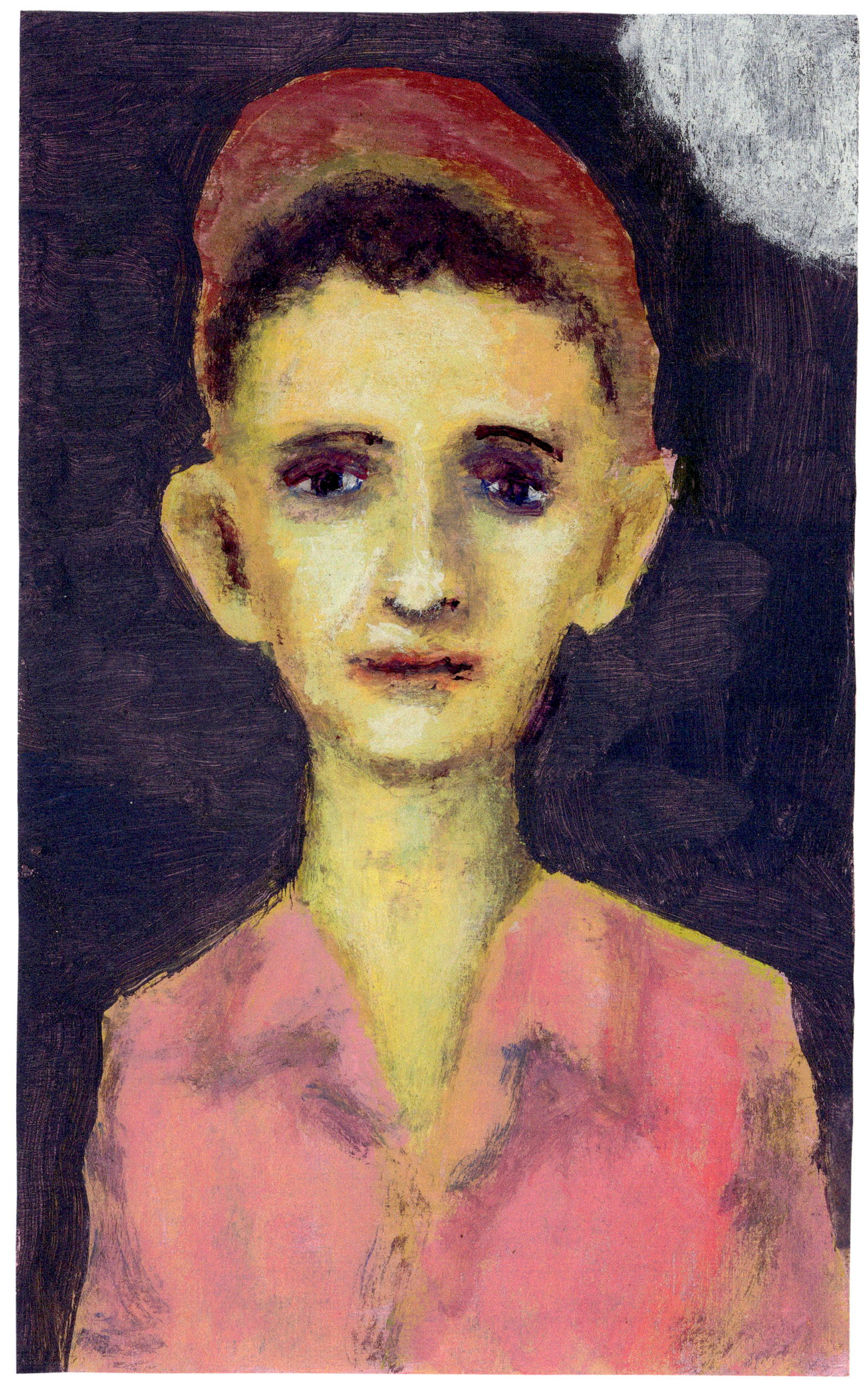

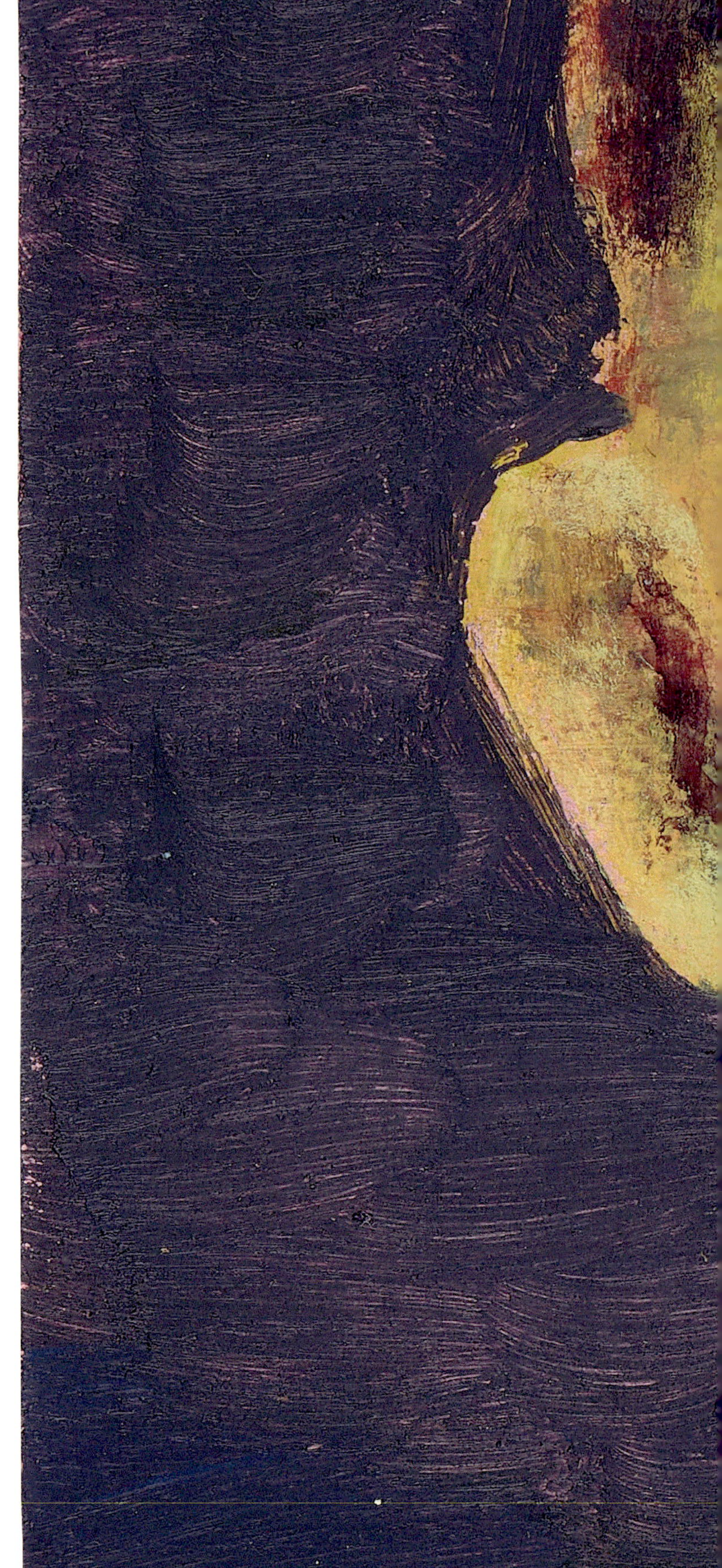

Night, 2024 (detail)

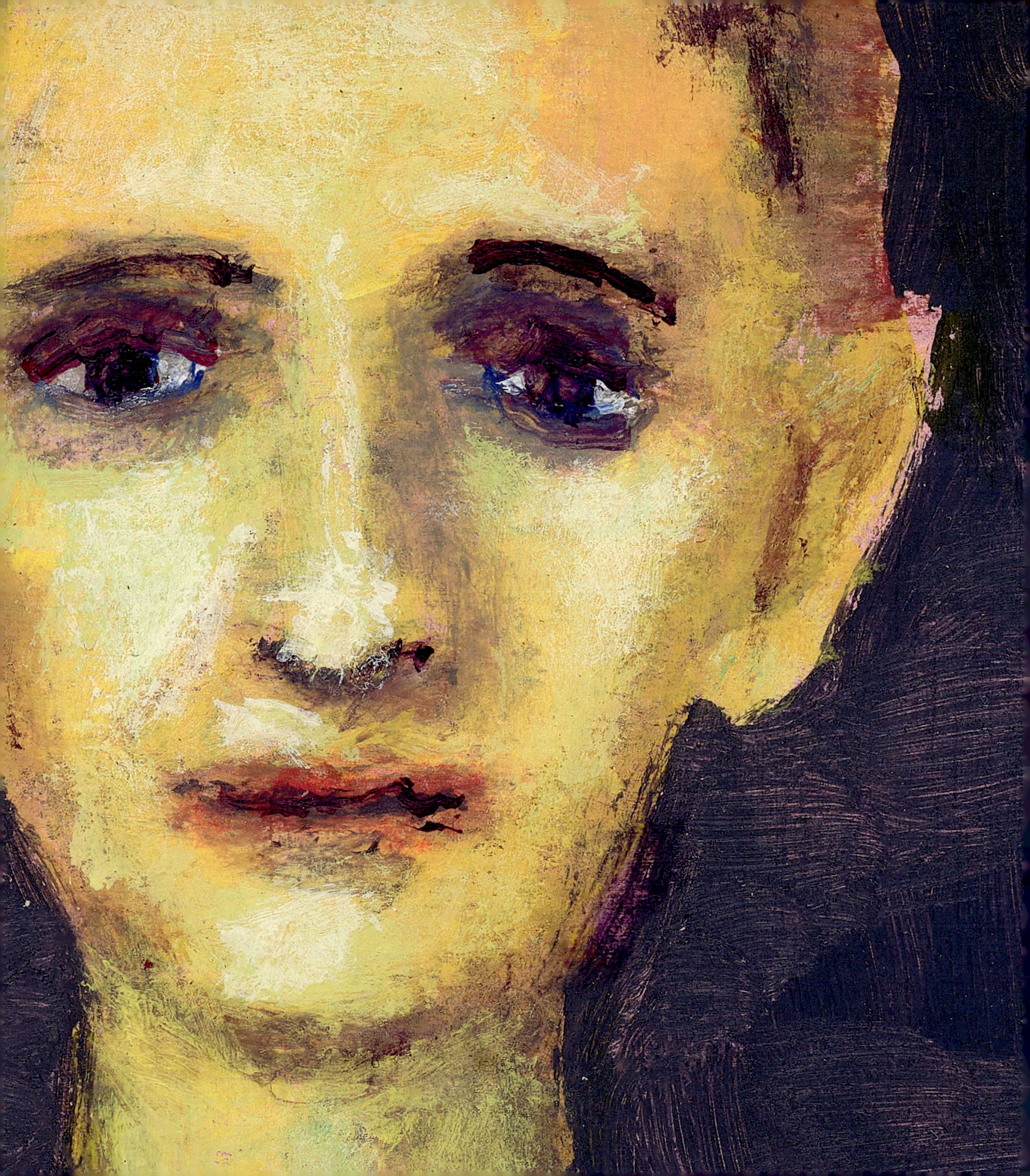

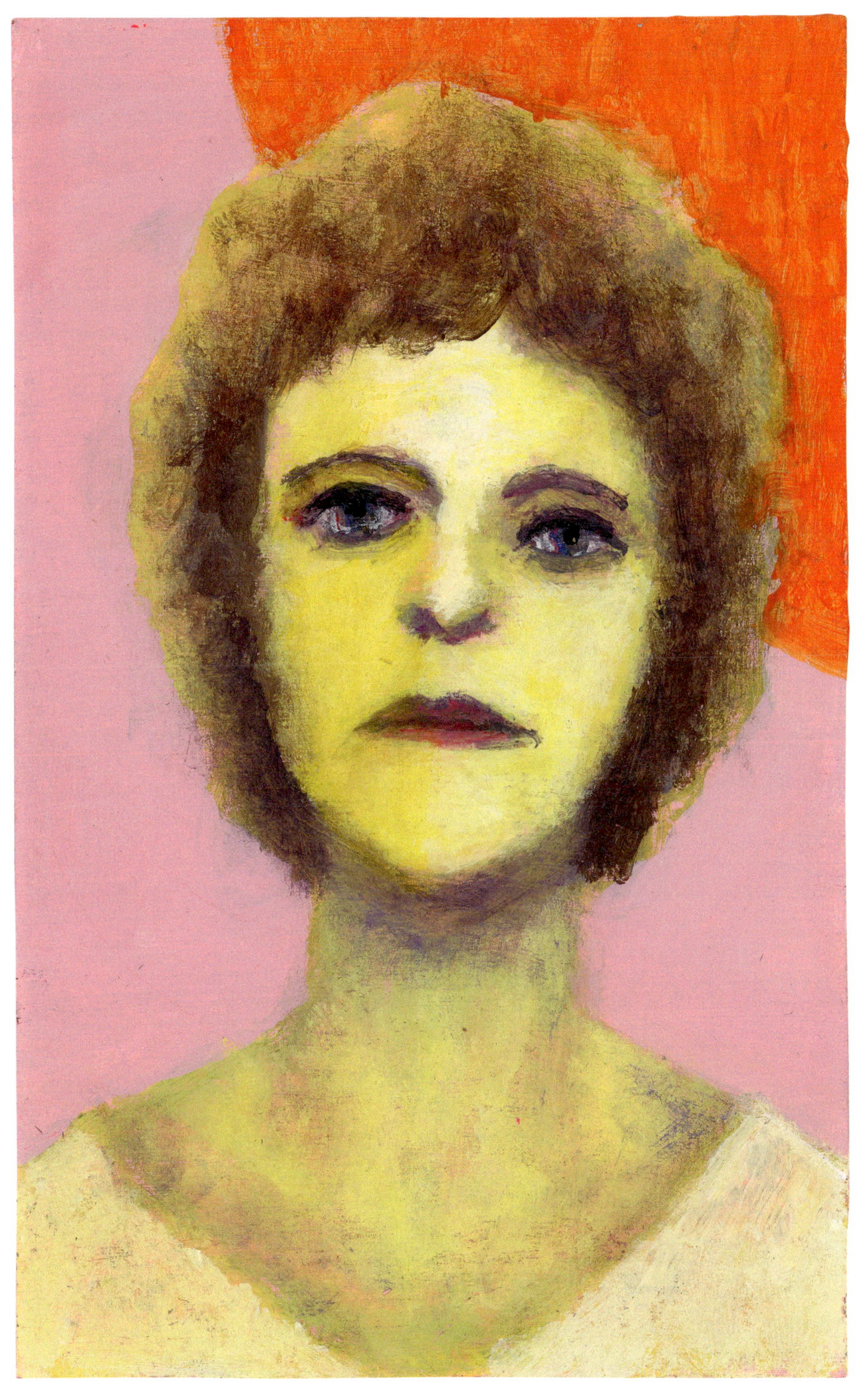

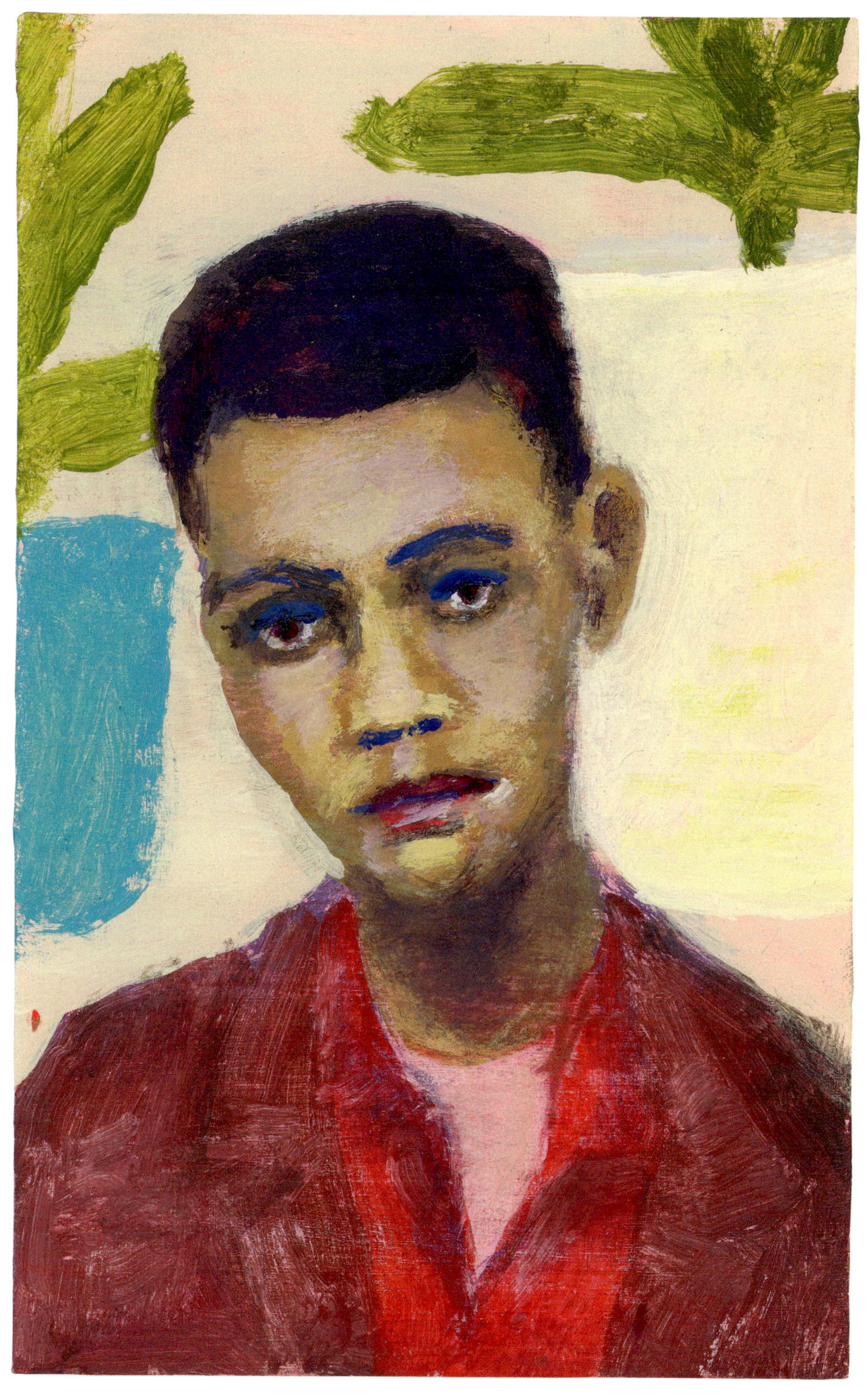

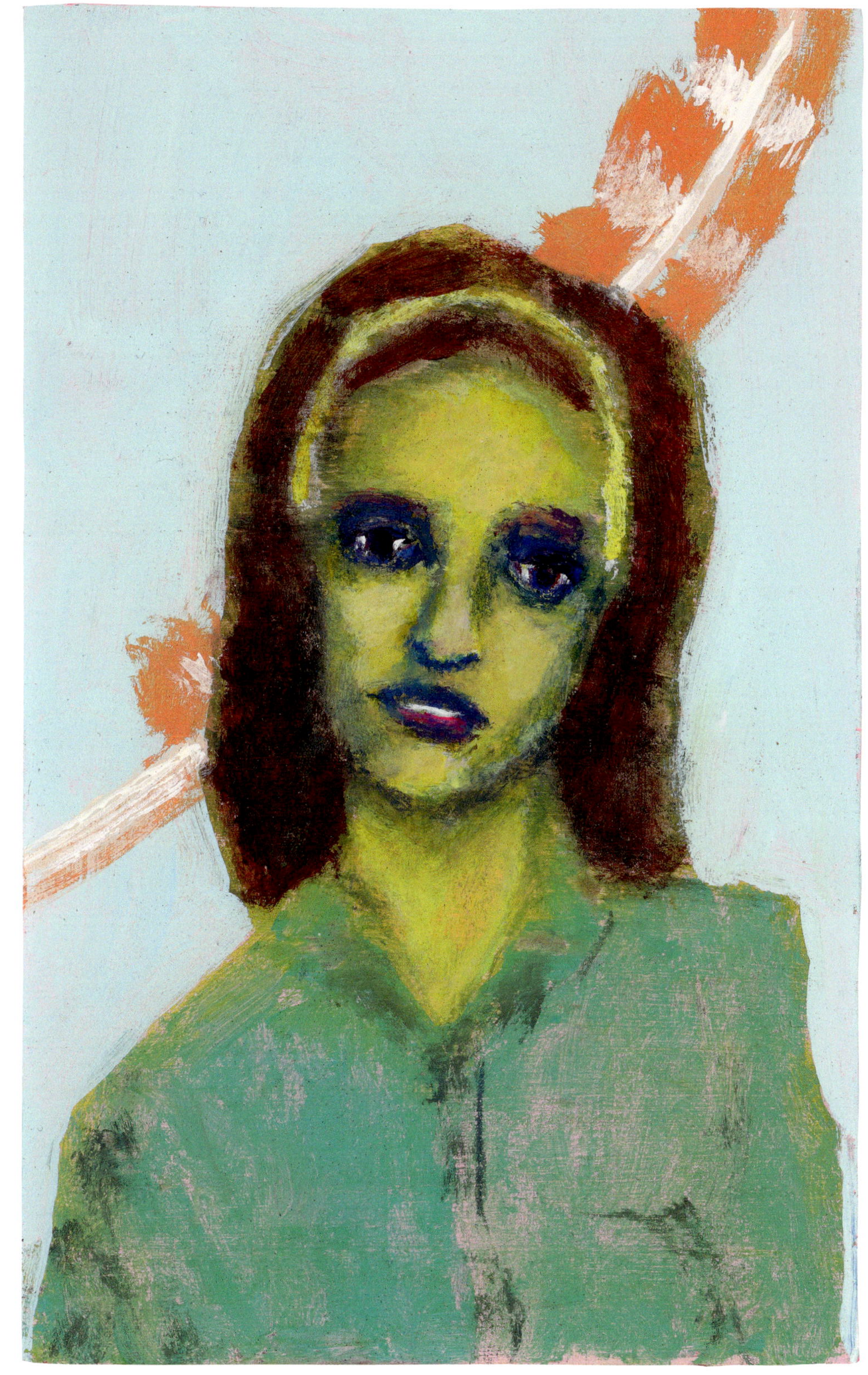

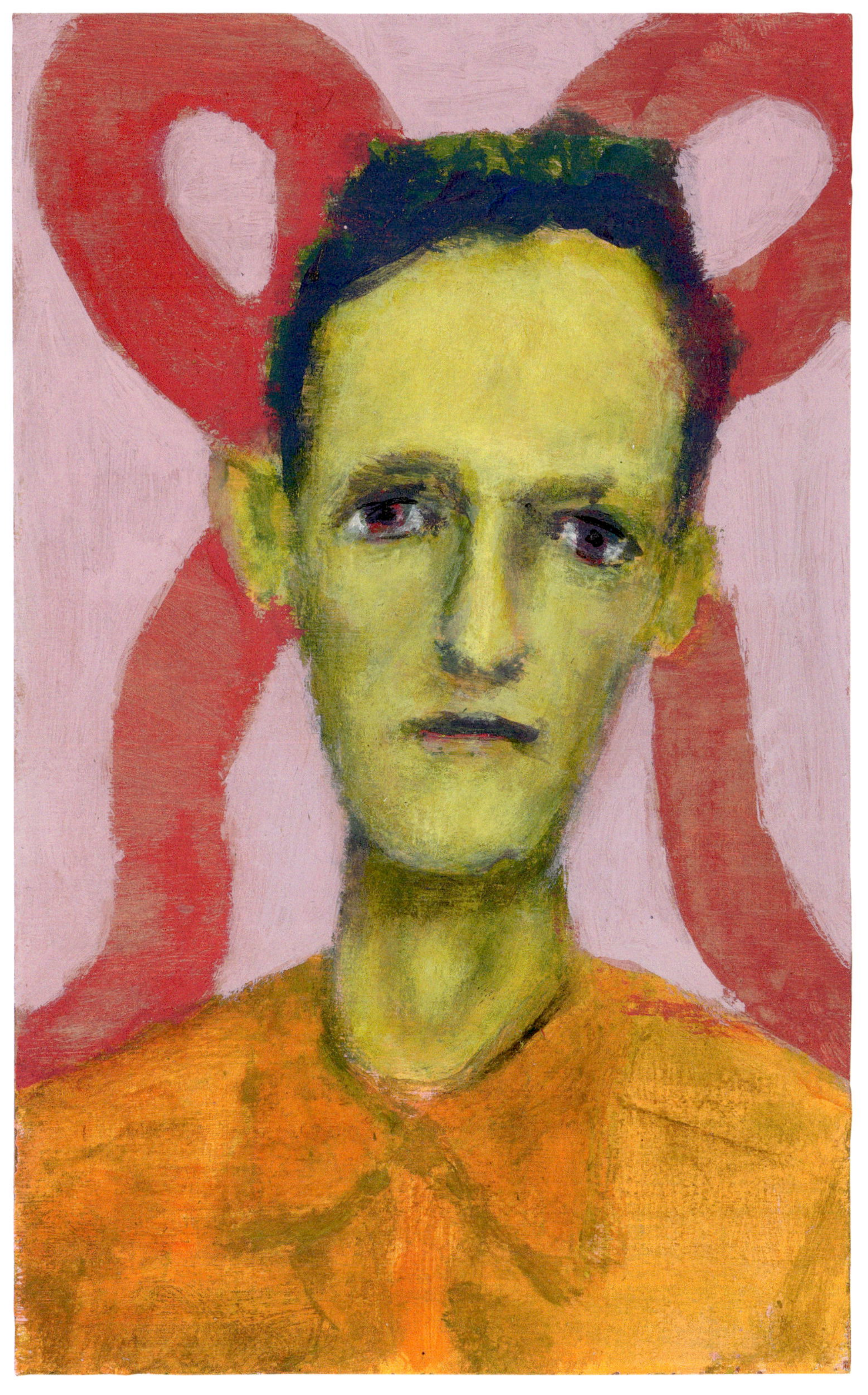

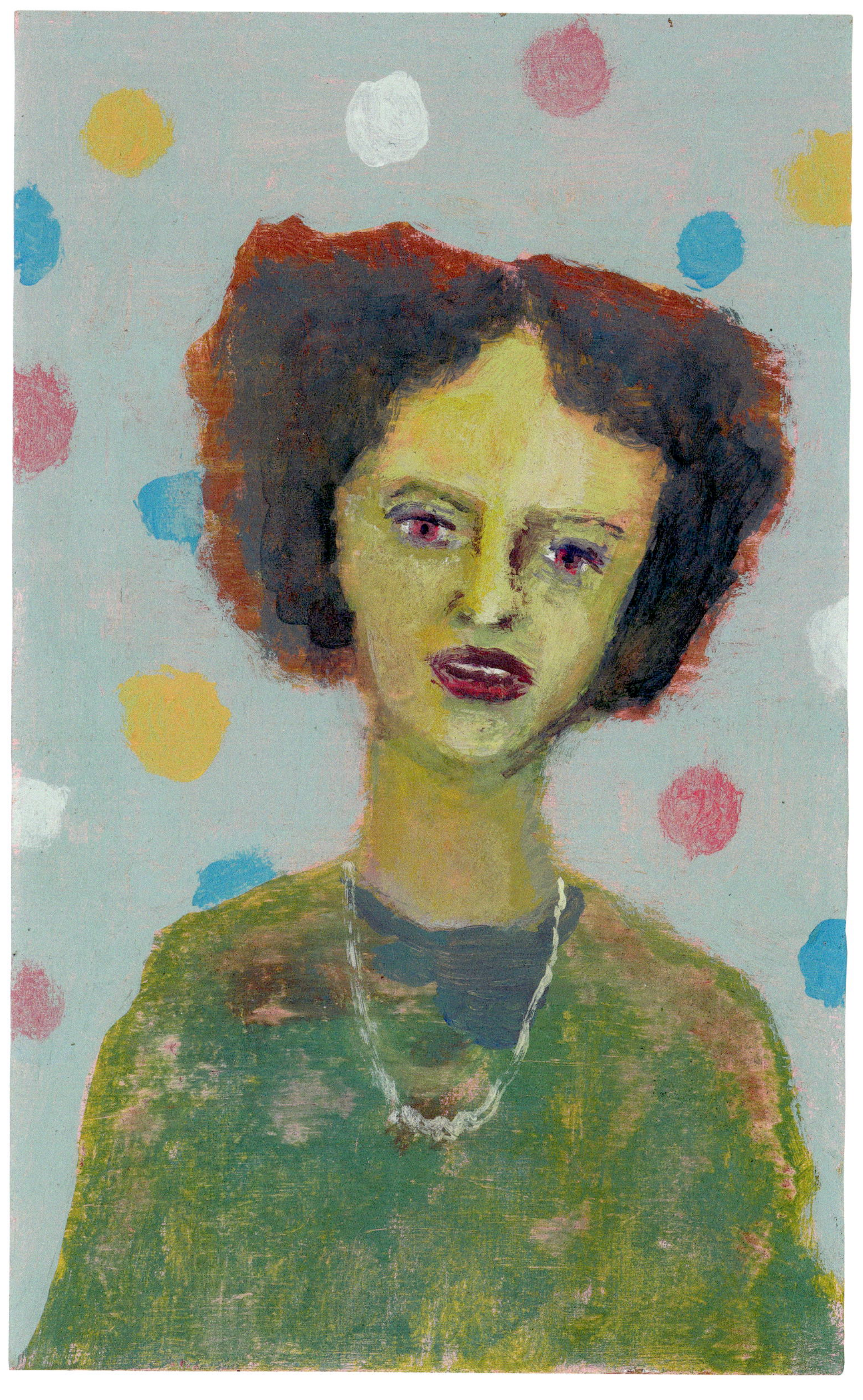

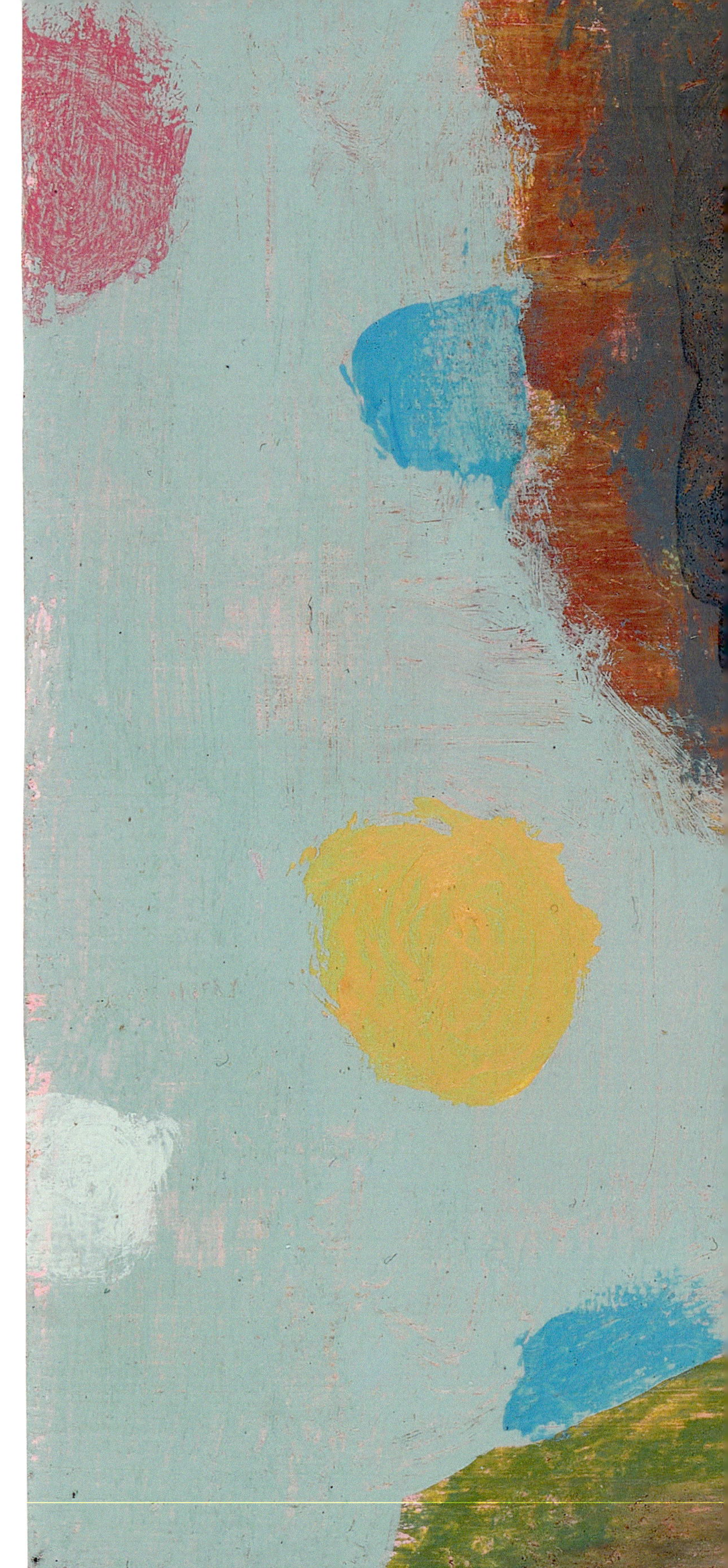

Spots, 2024 (detail)

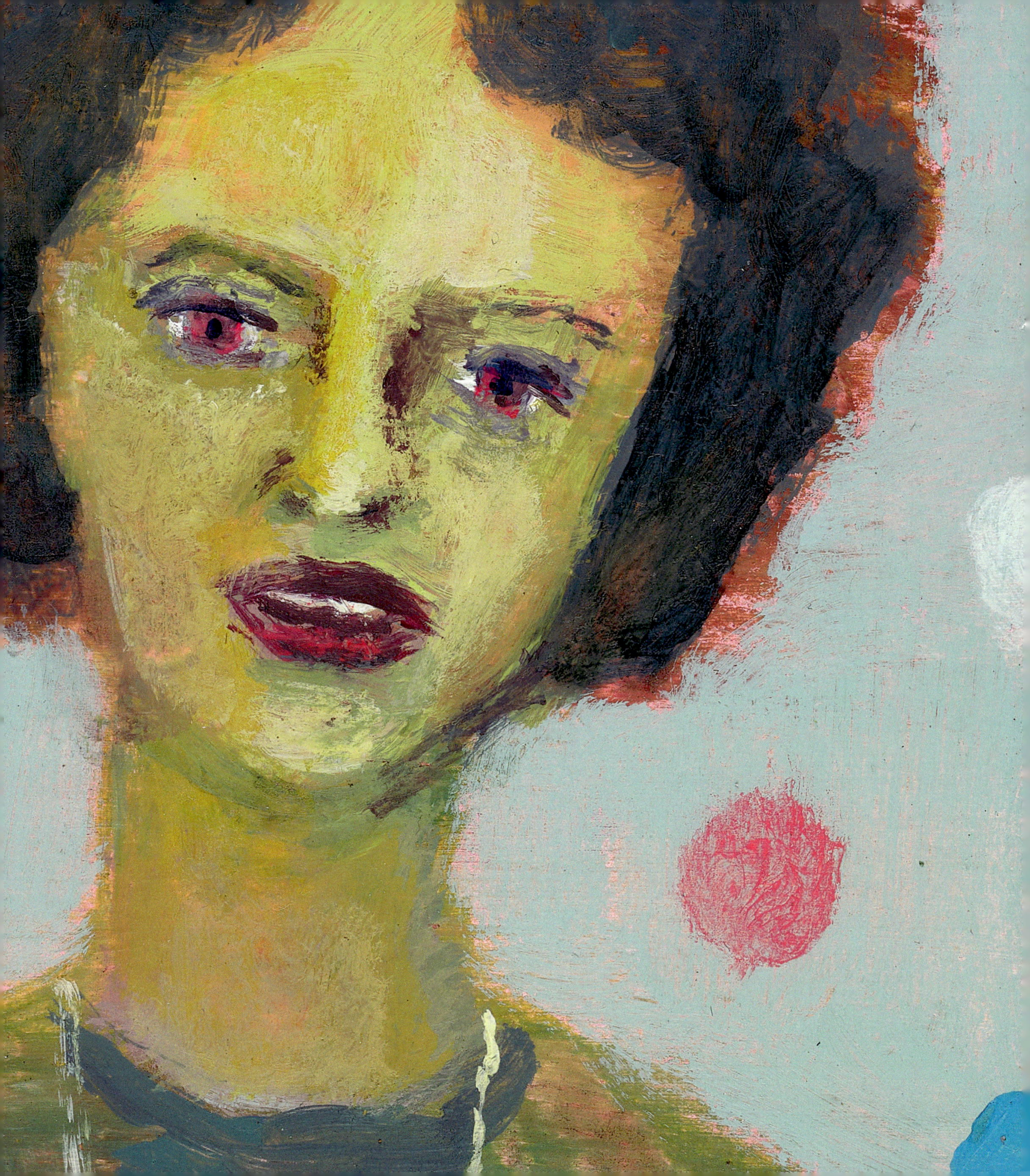

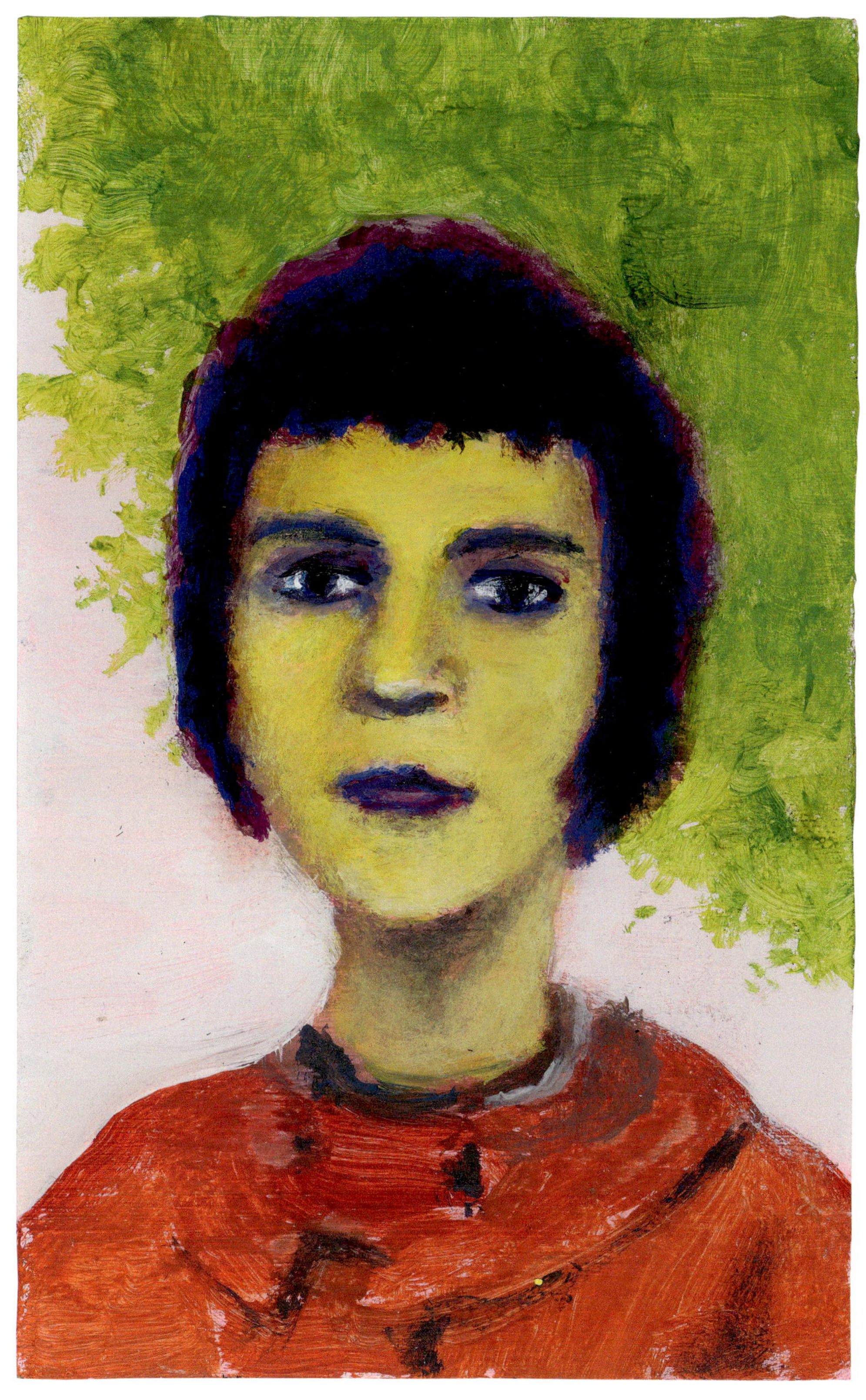

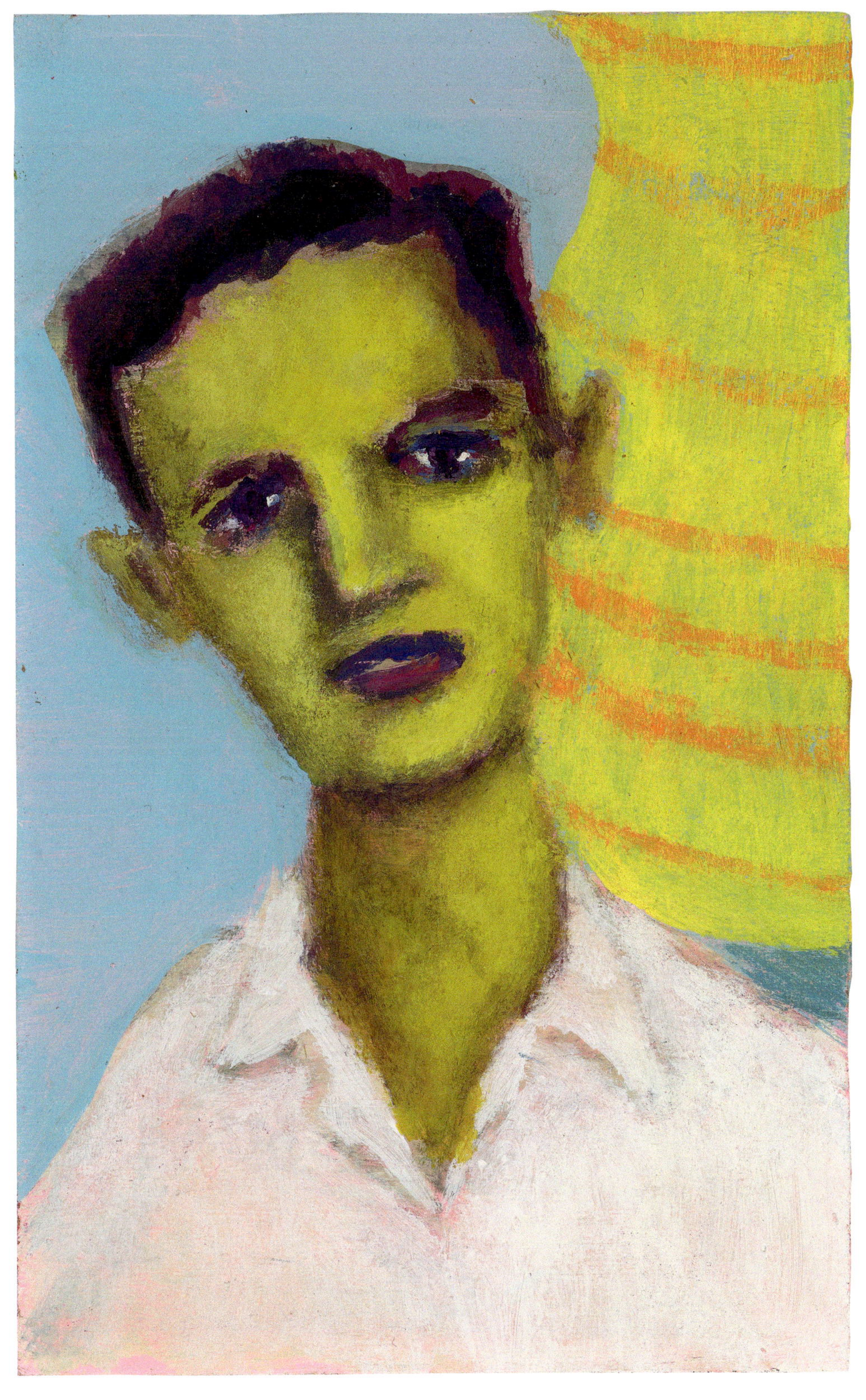

Watermelon, 2024

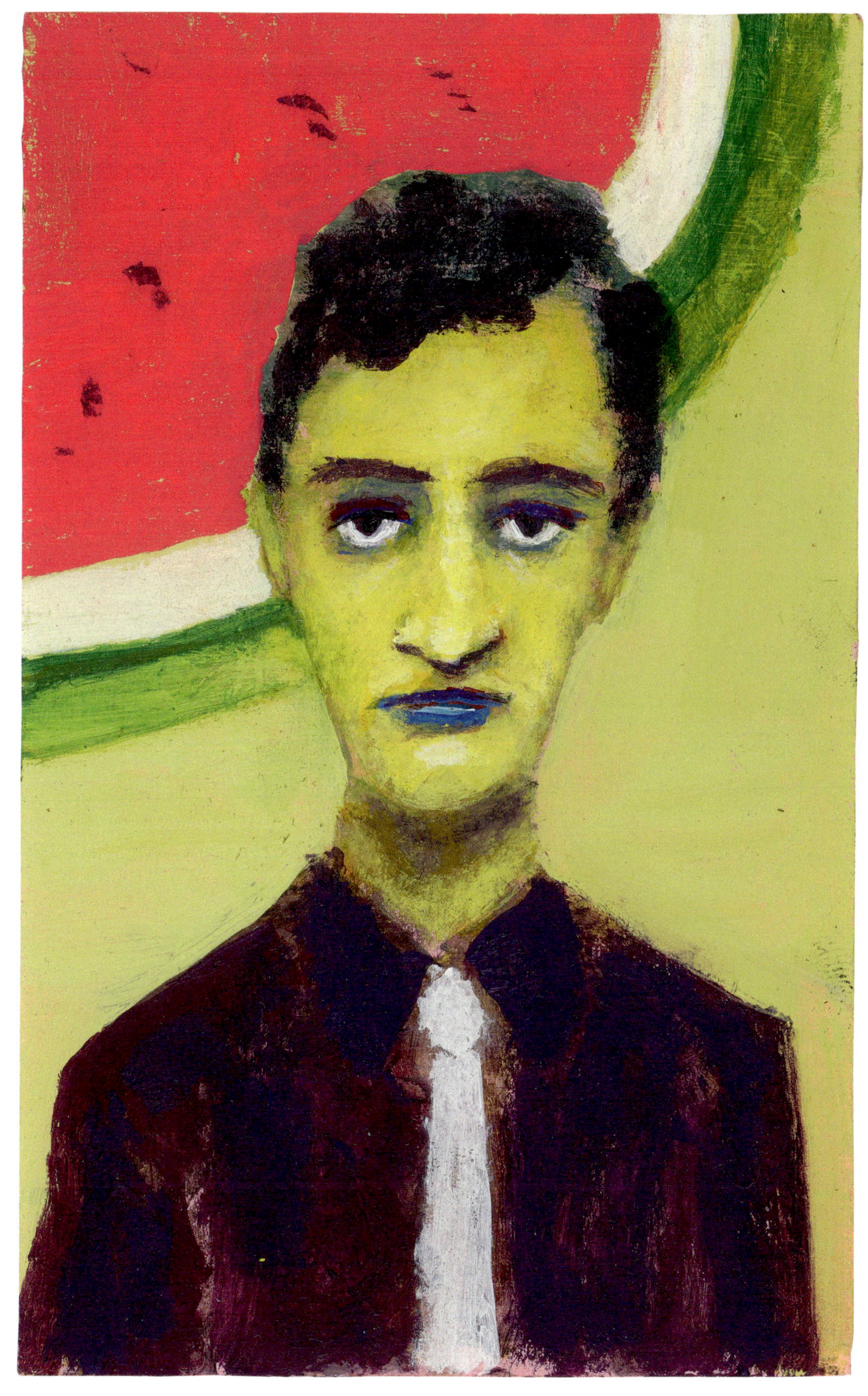

Xylophone, 2024

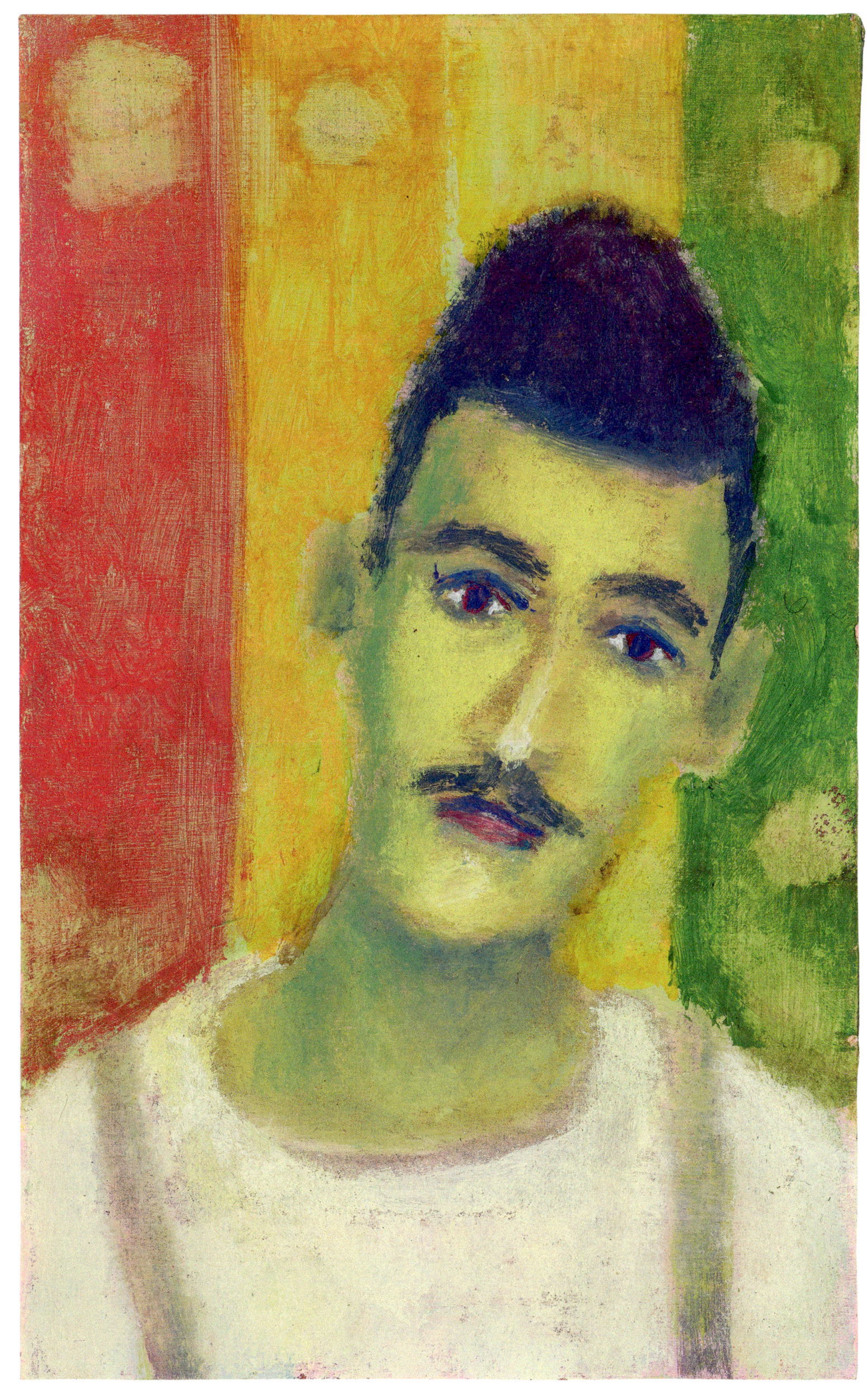

Xylophone, 2024 (detail)

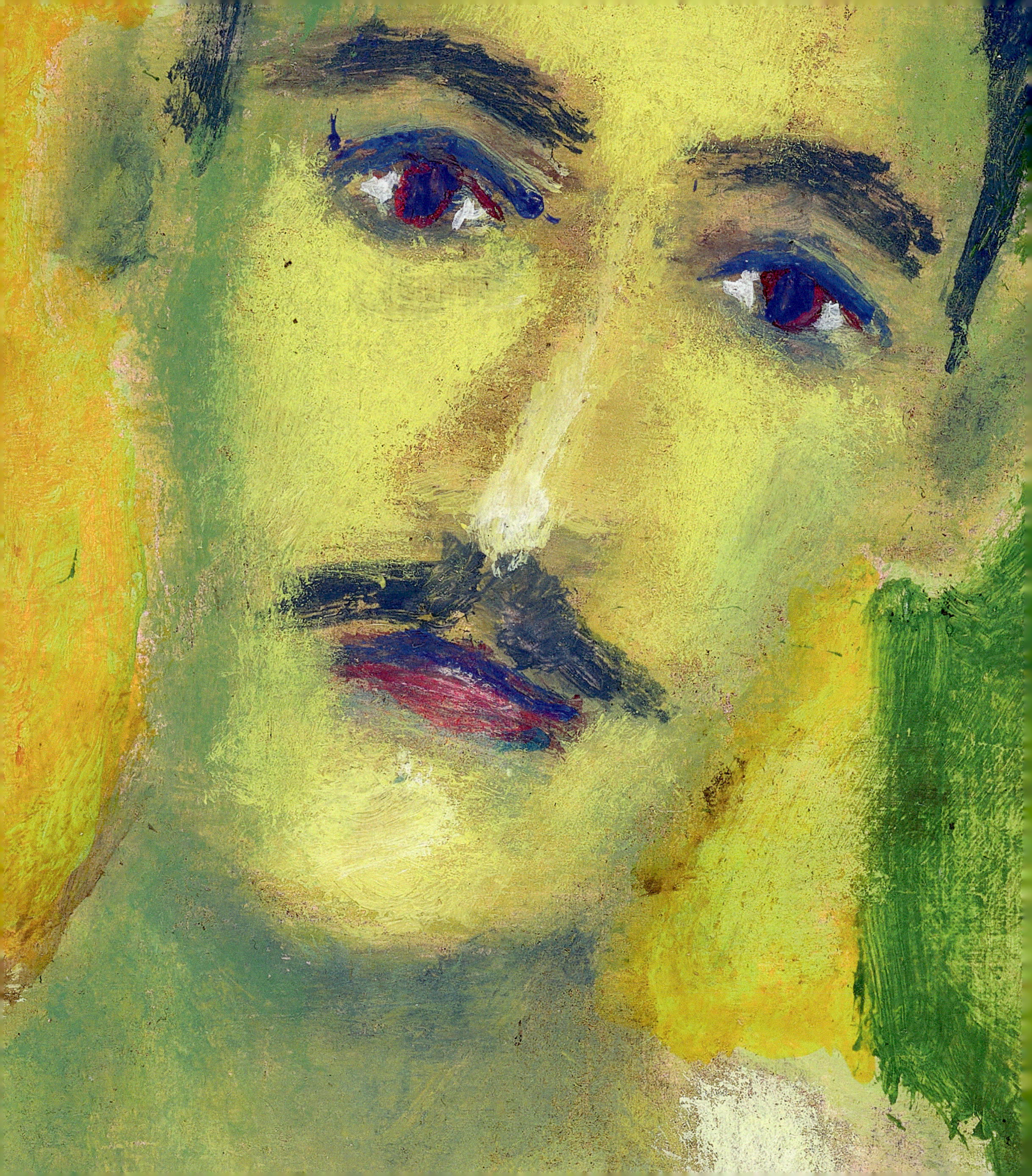

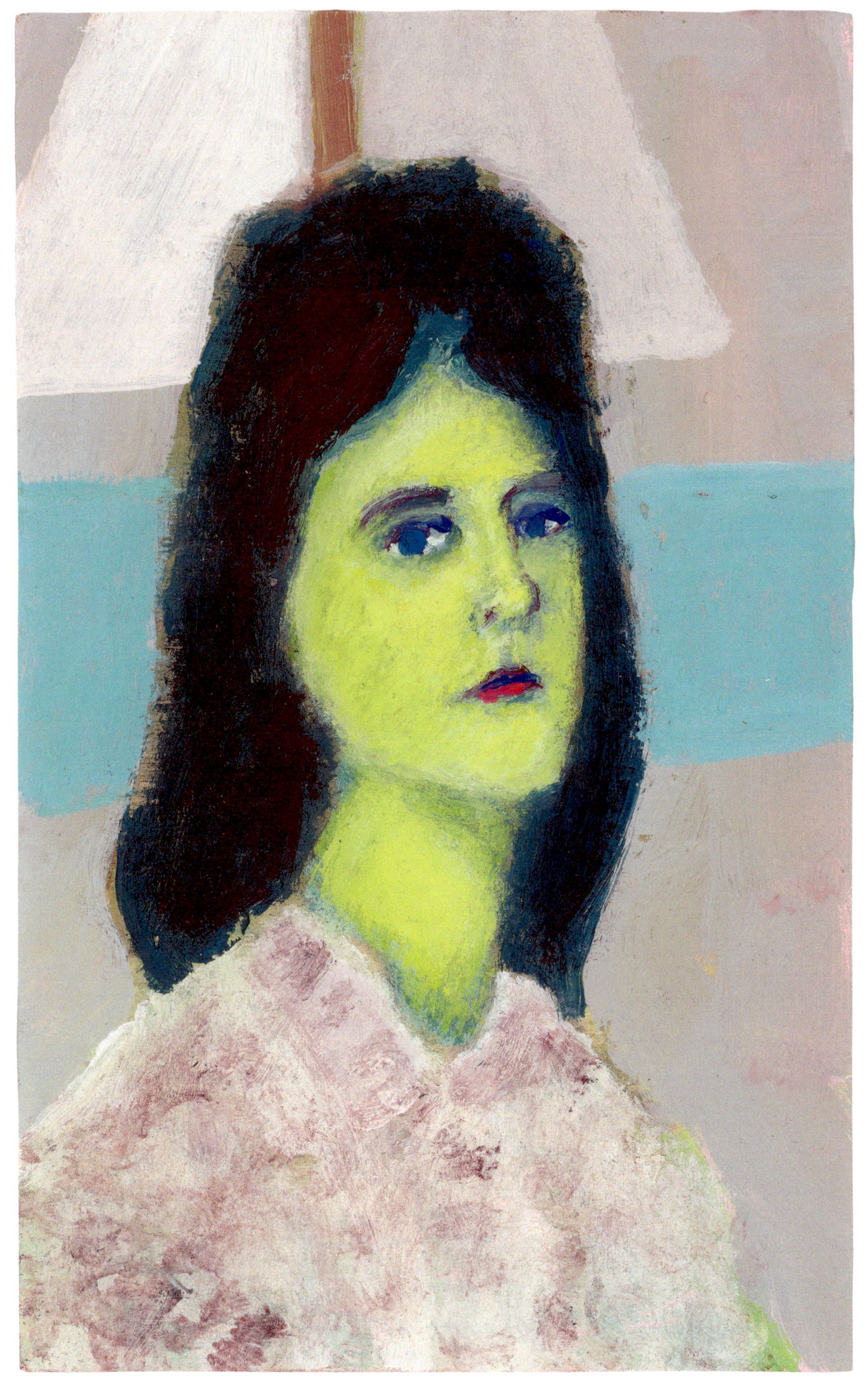

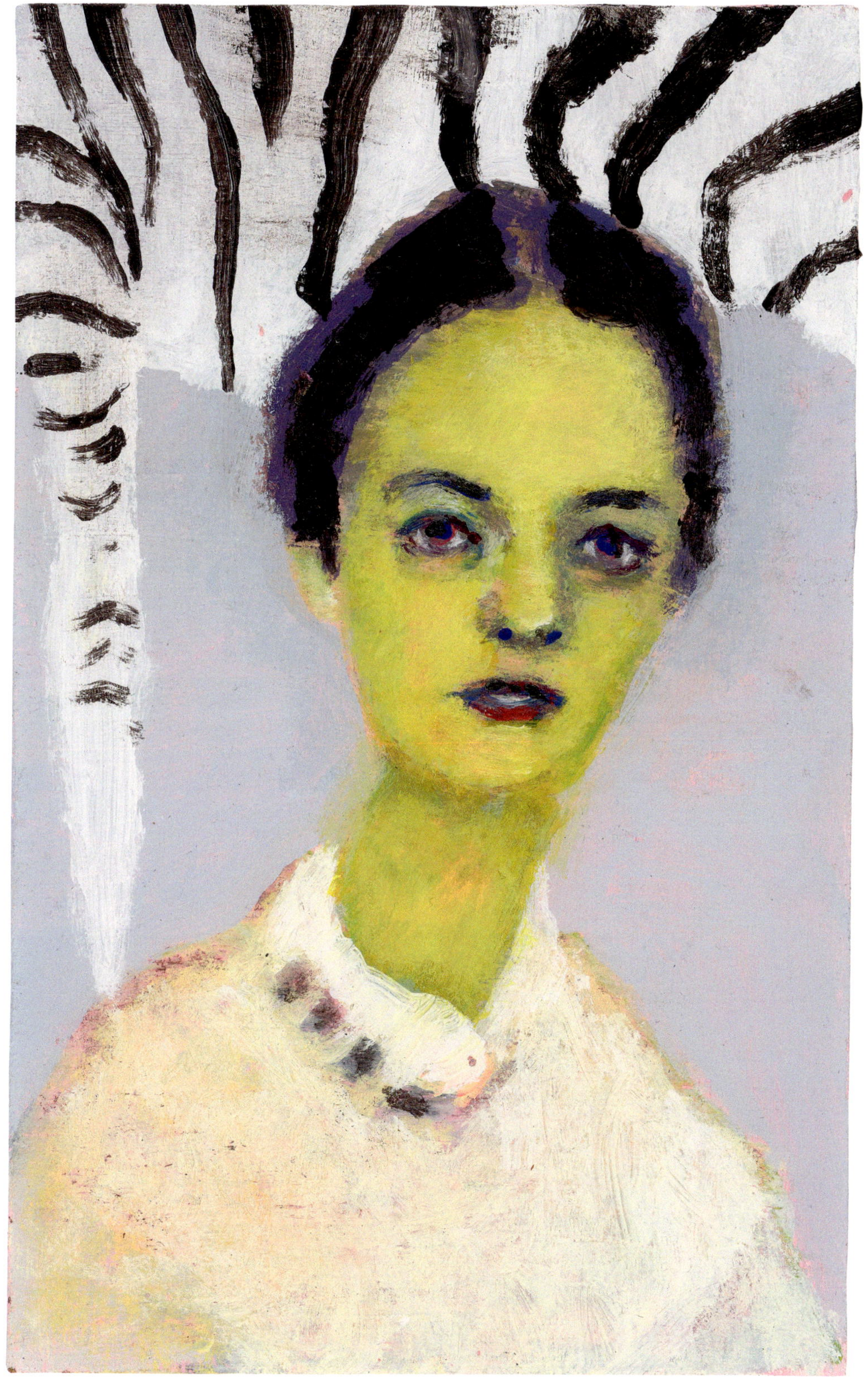

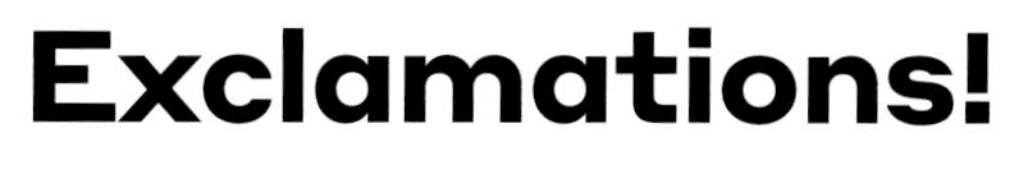

Exclamations!

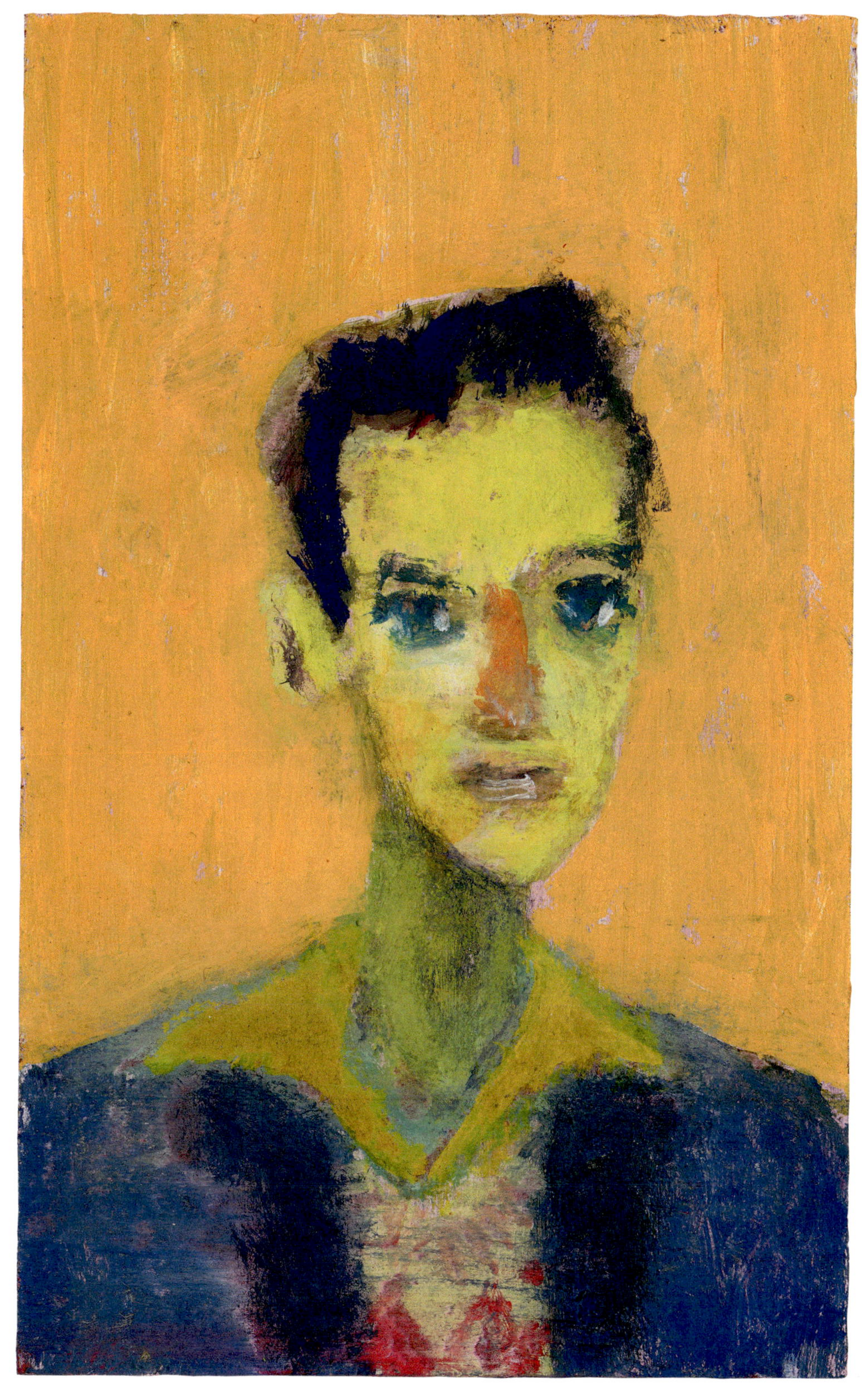

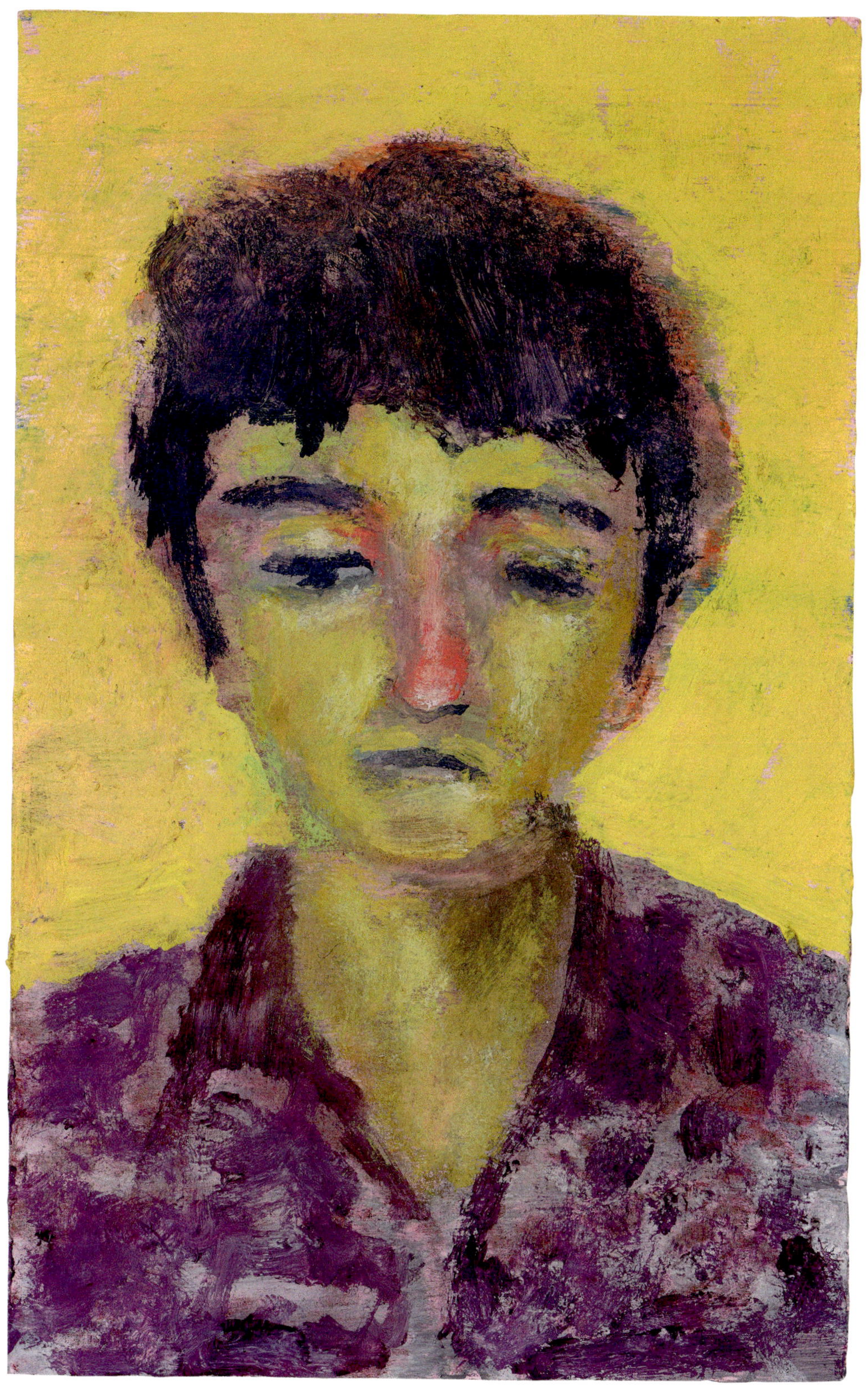

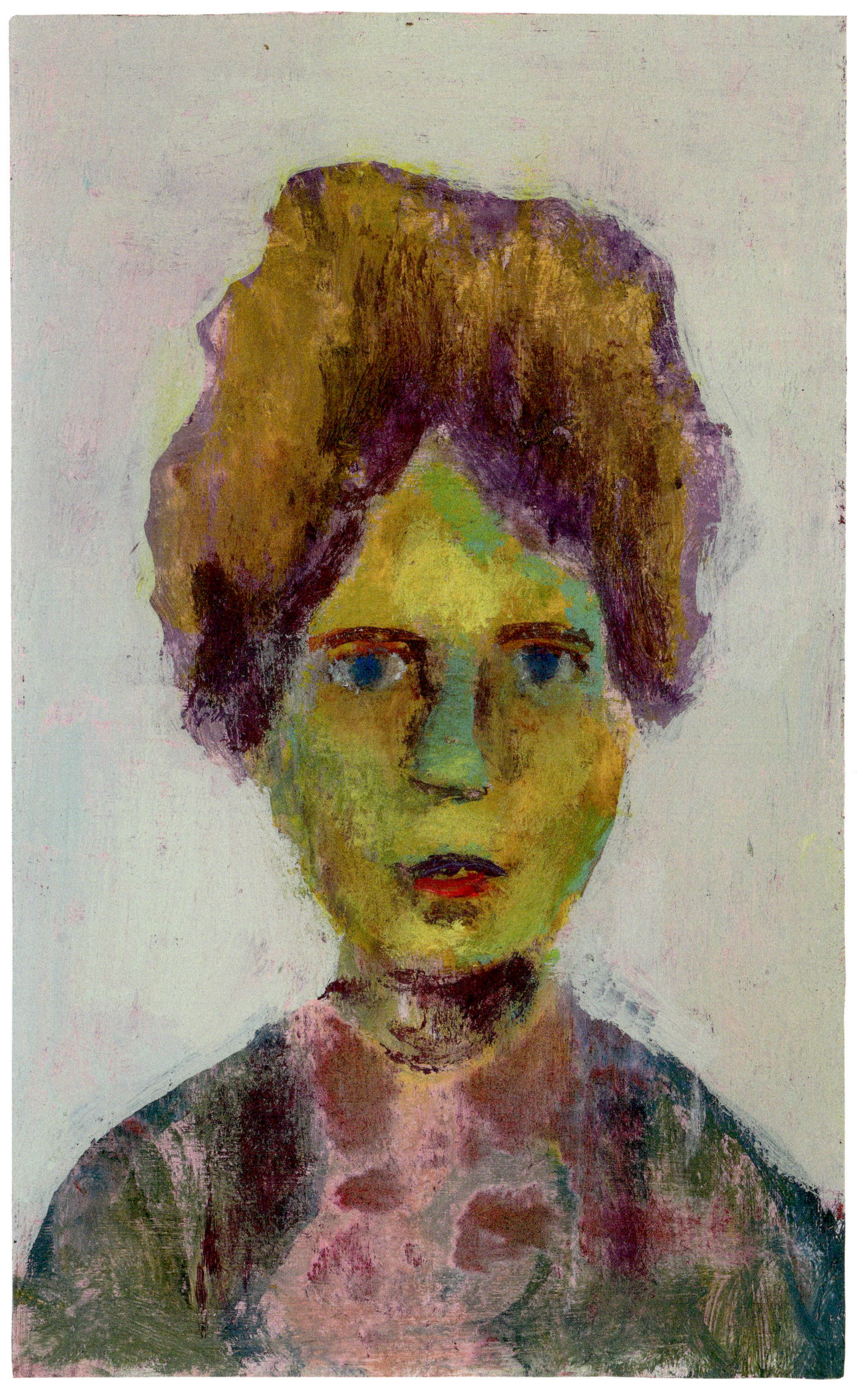

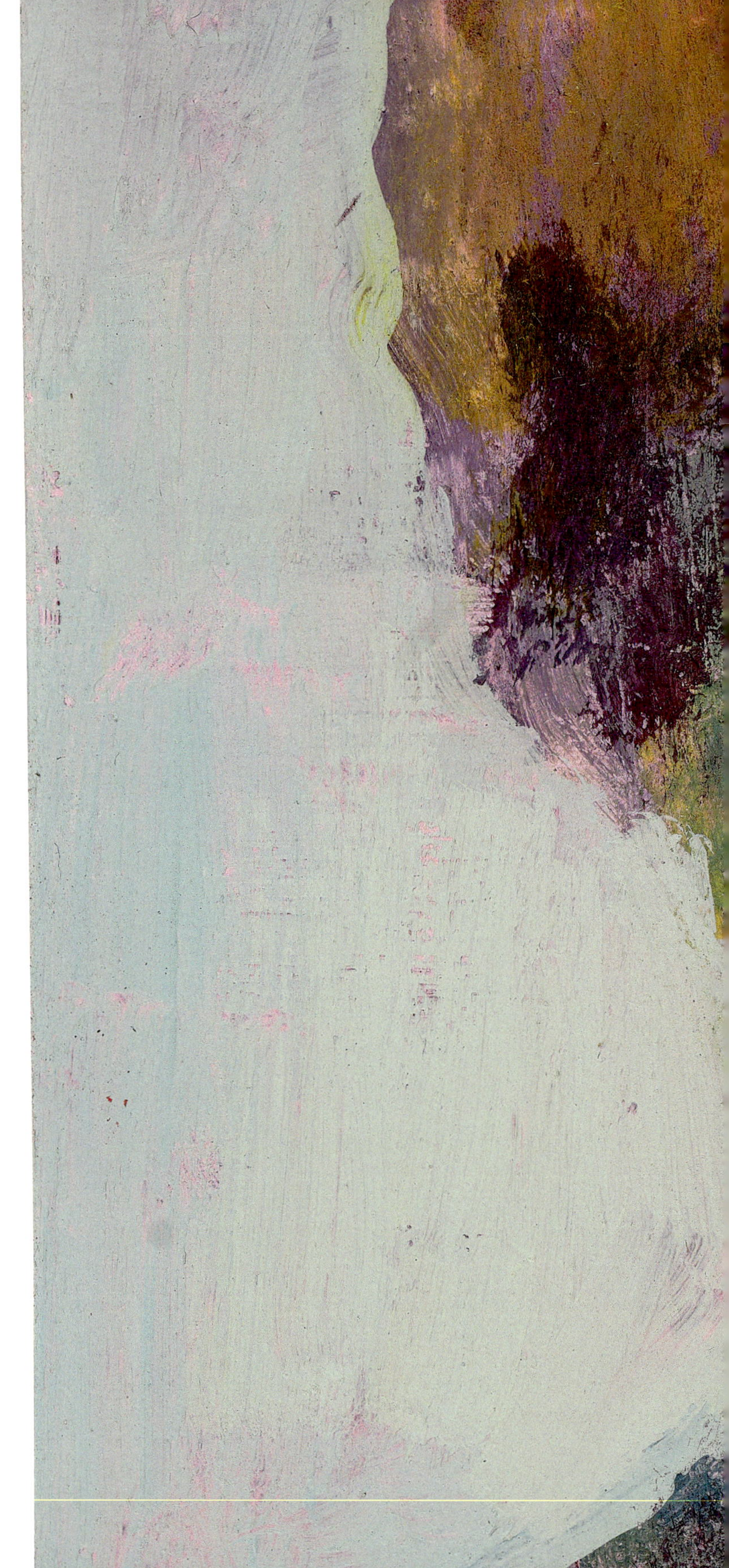

Crikey!, 2023 (detail)

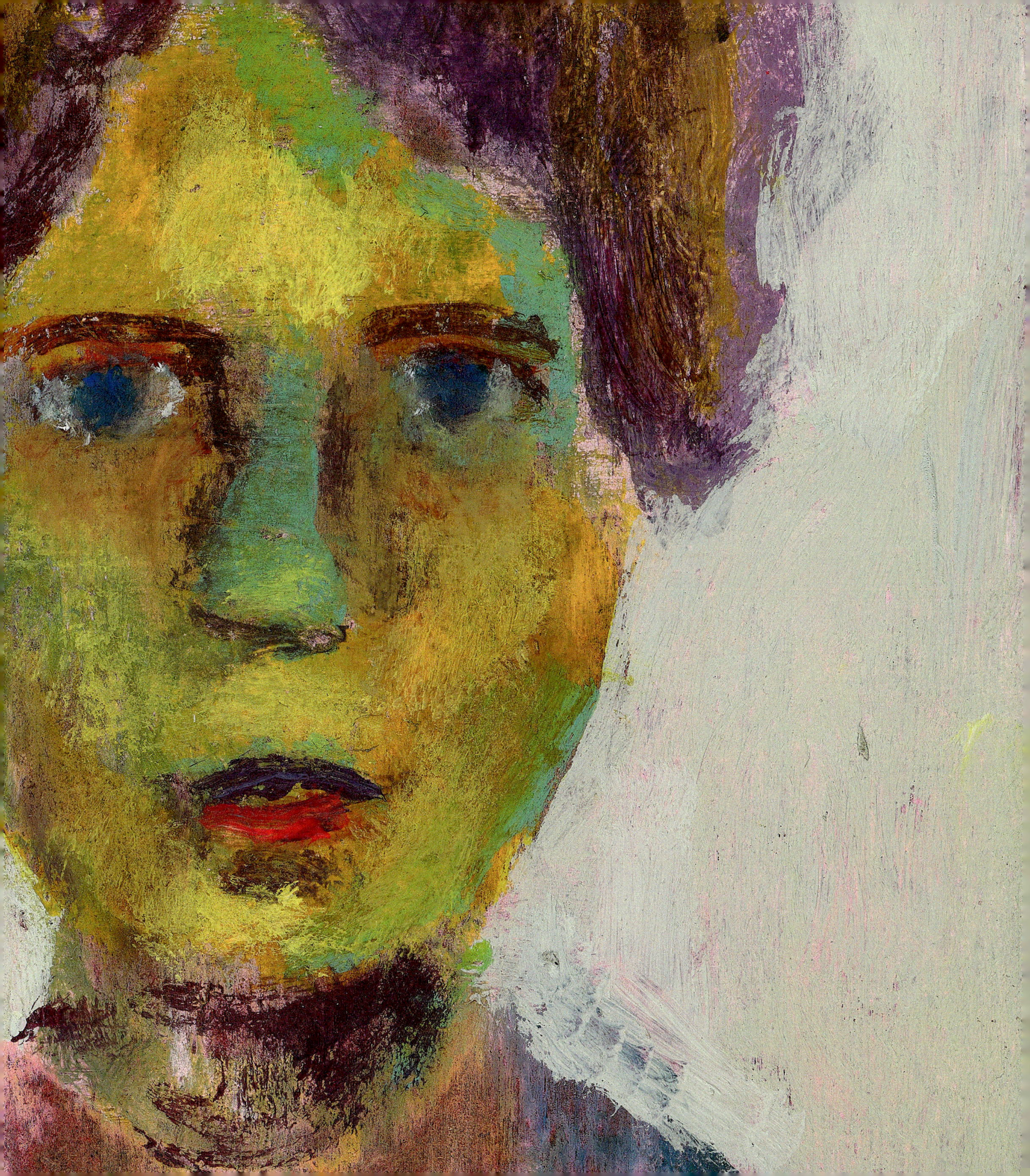

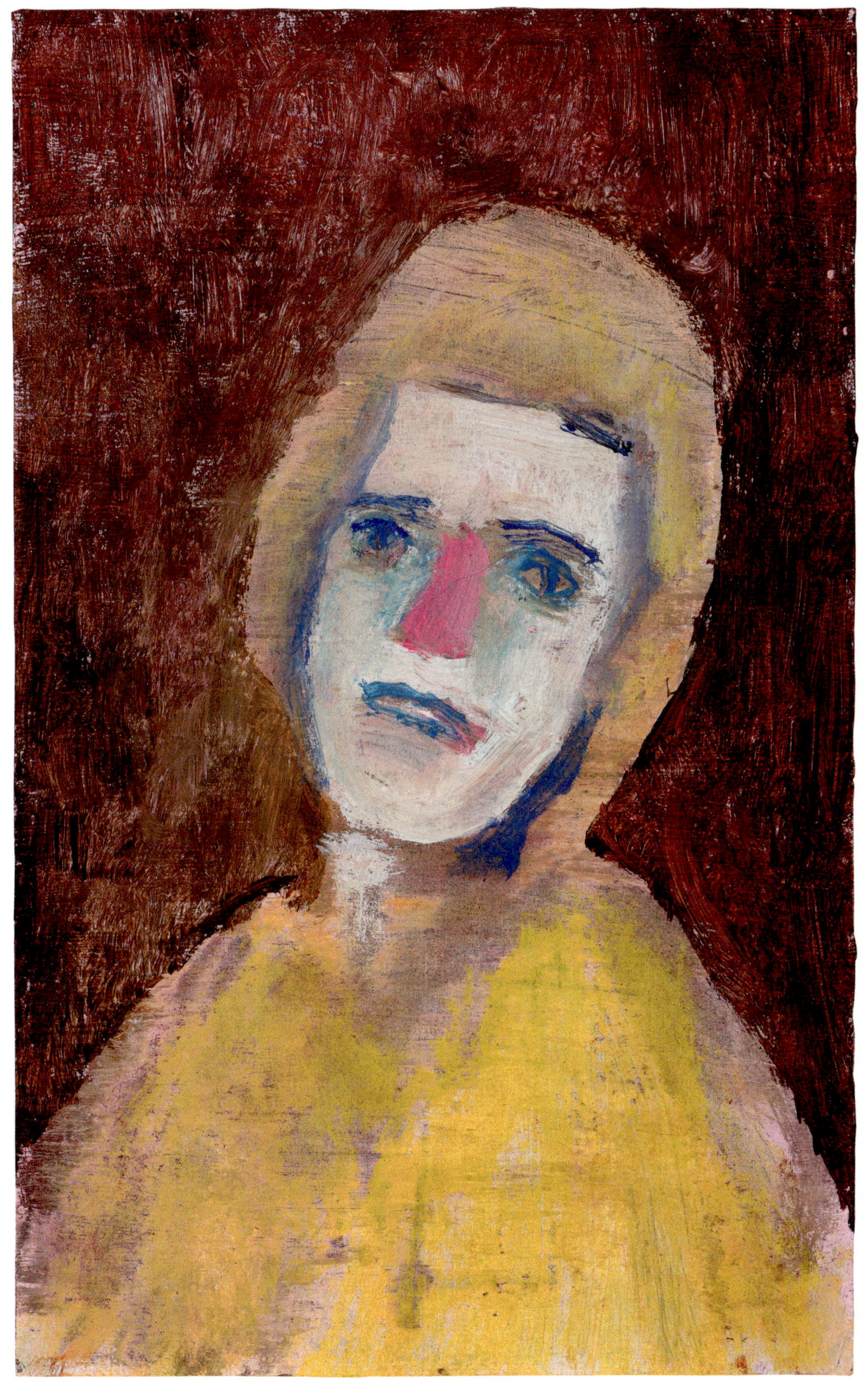

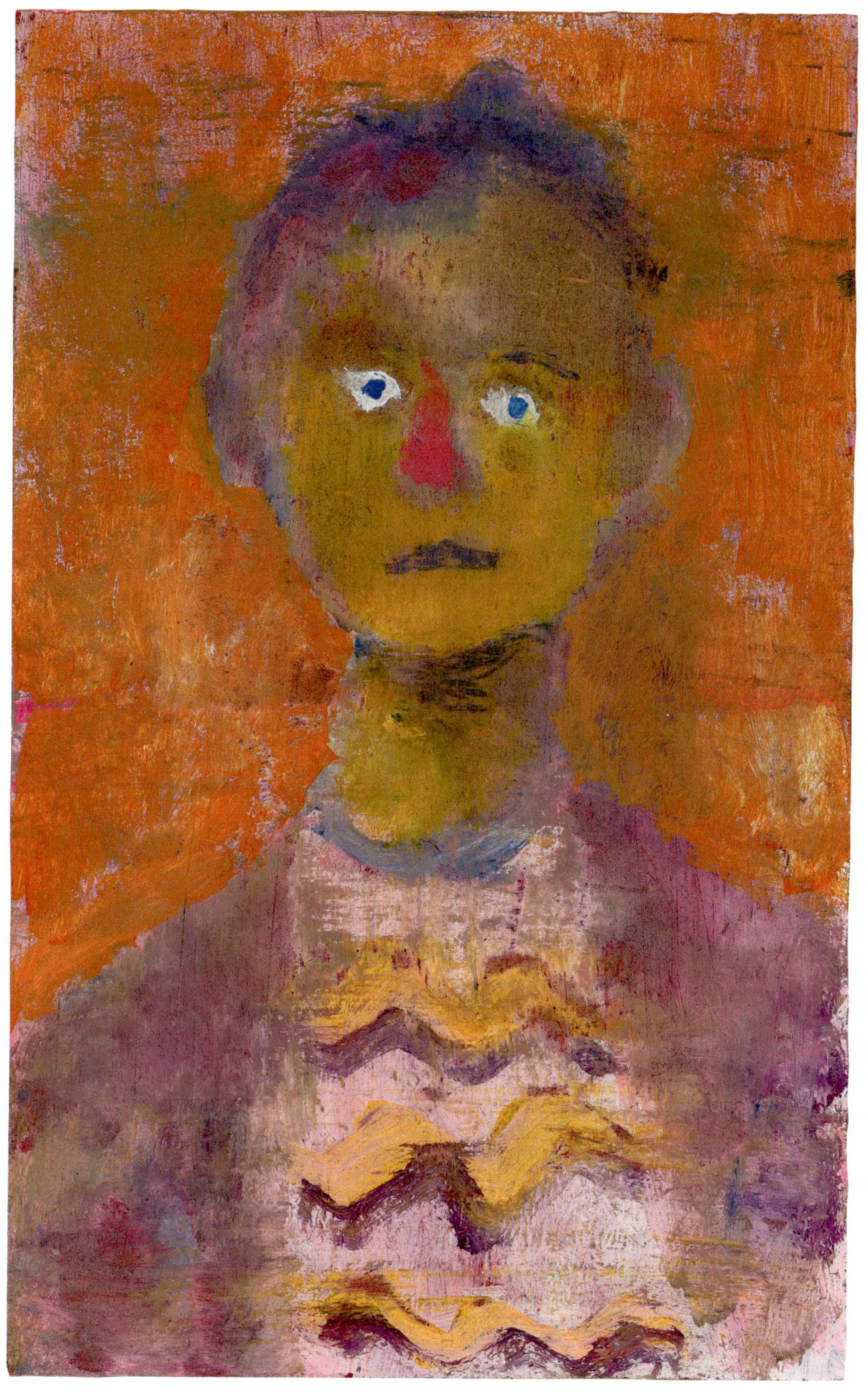

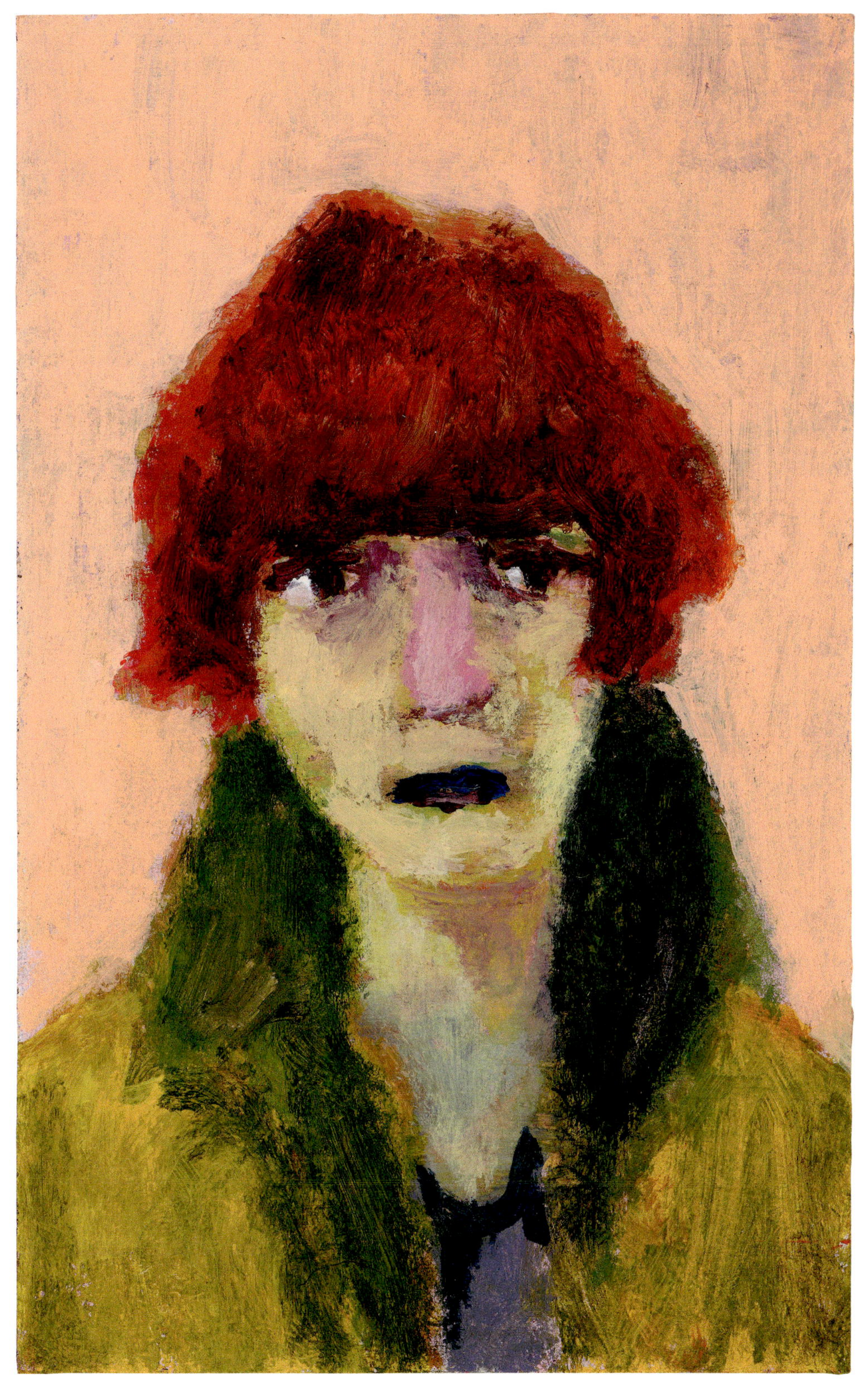

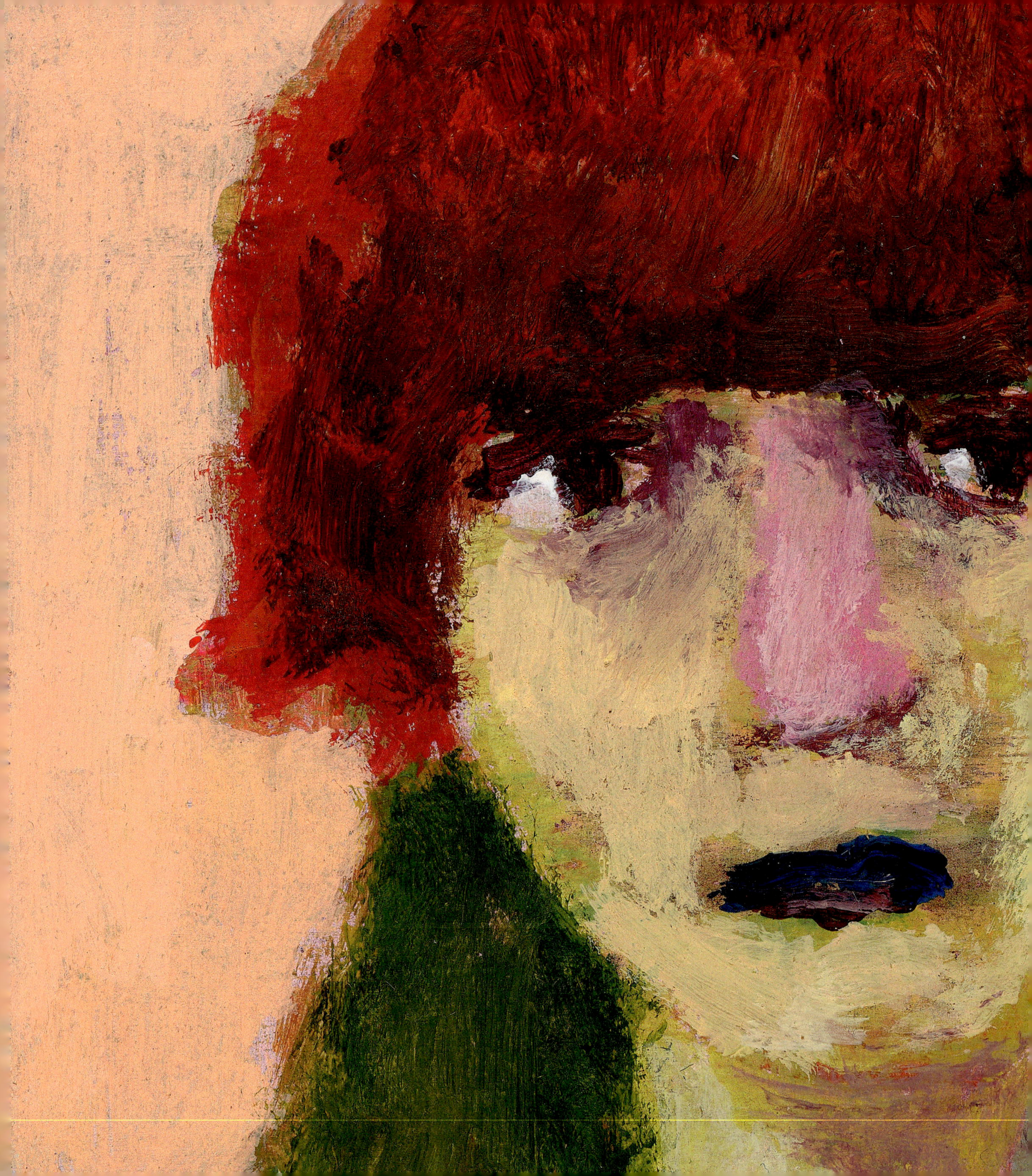

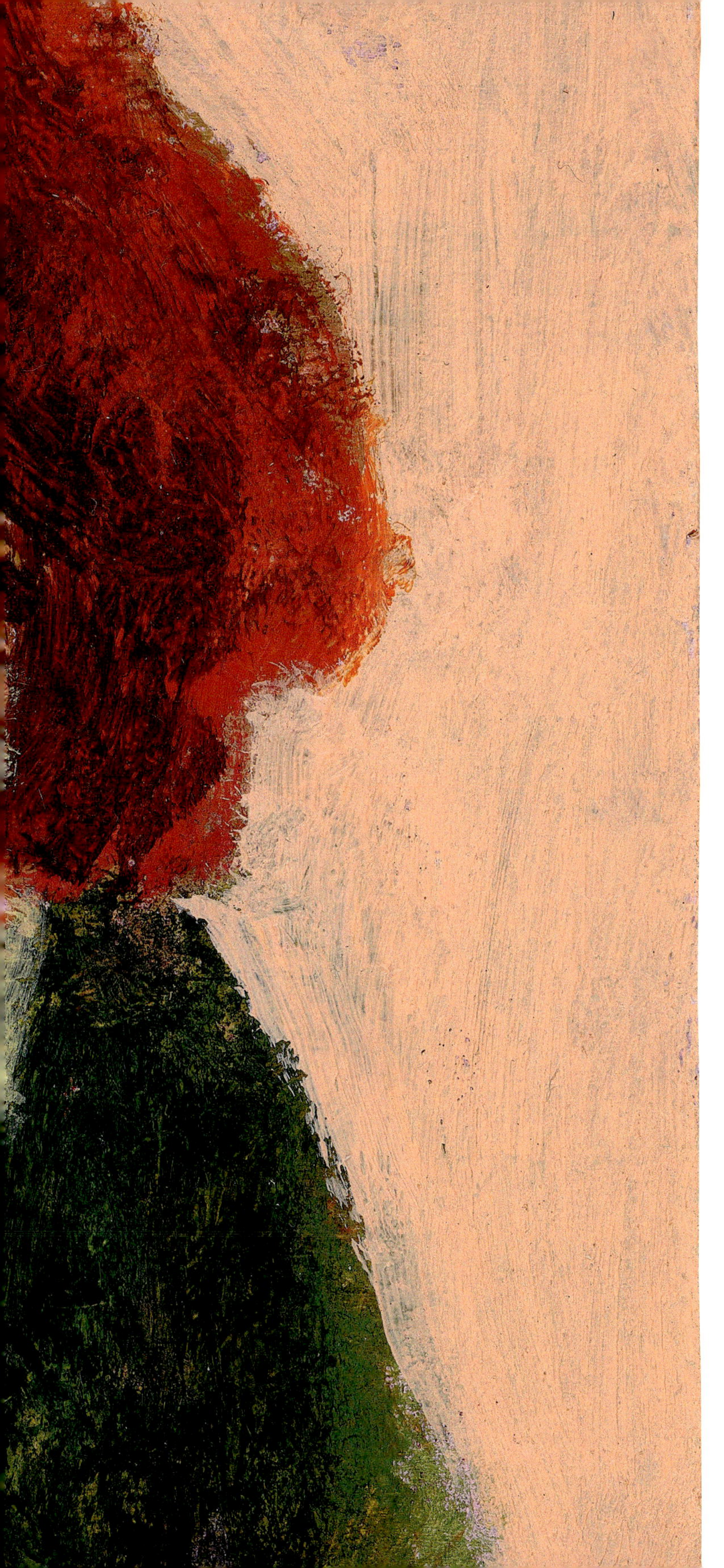

Forever!, 2023 (detail)

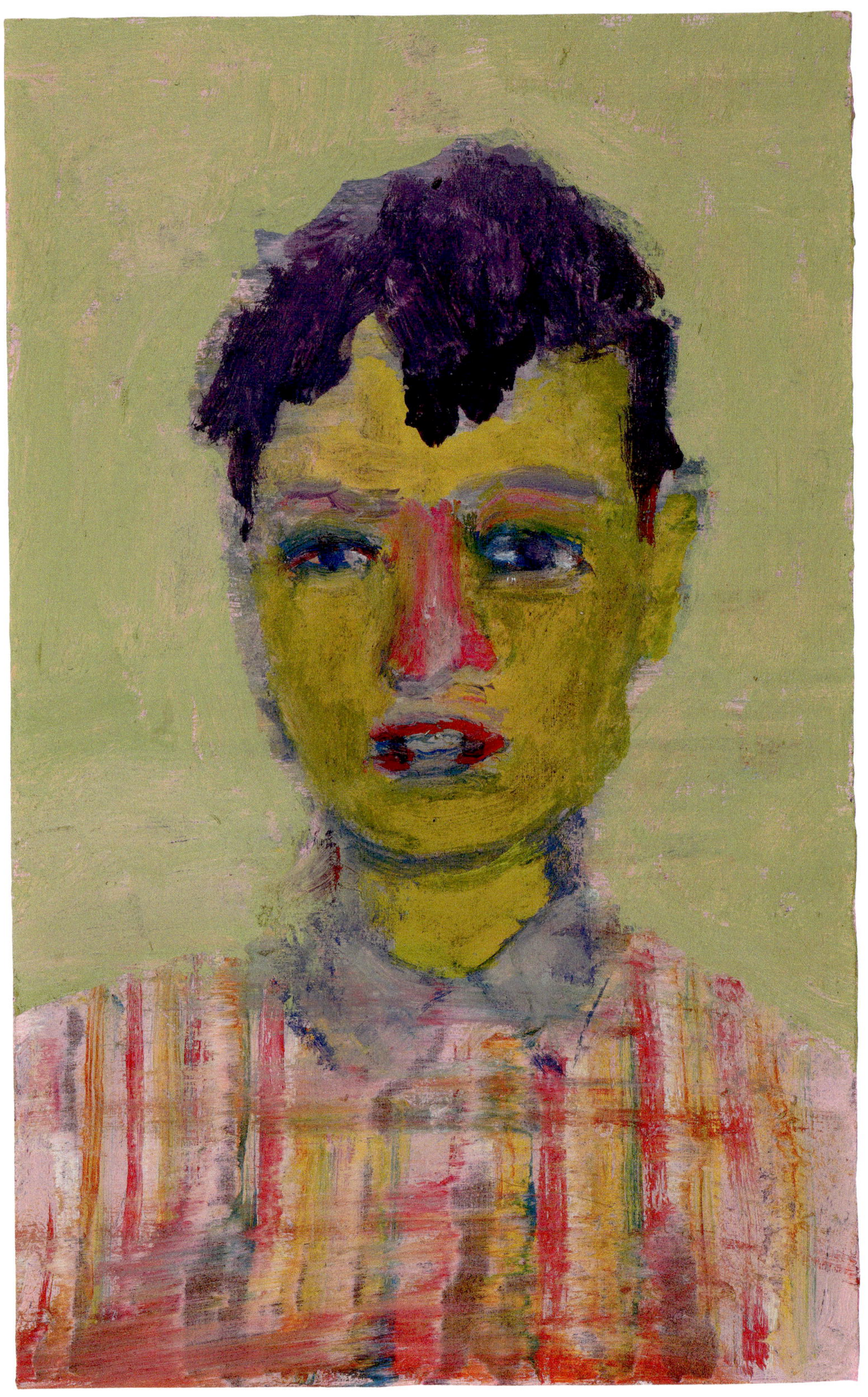

Goodness!, 2023

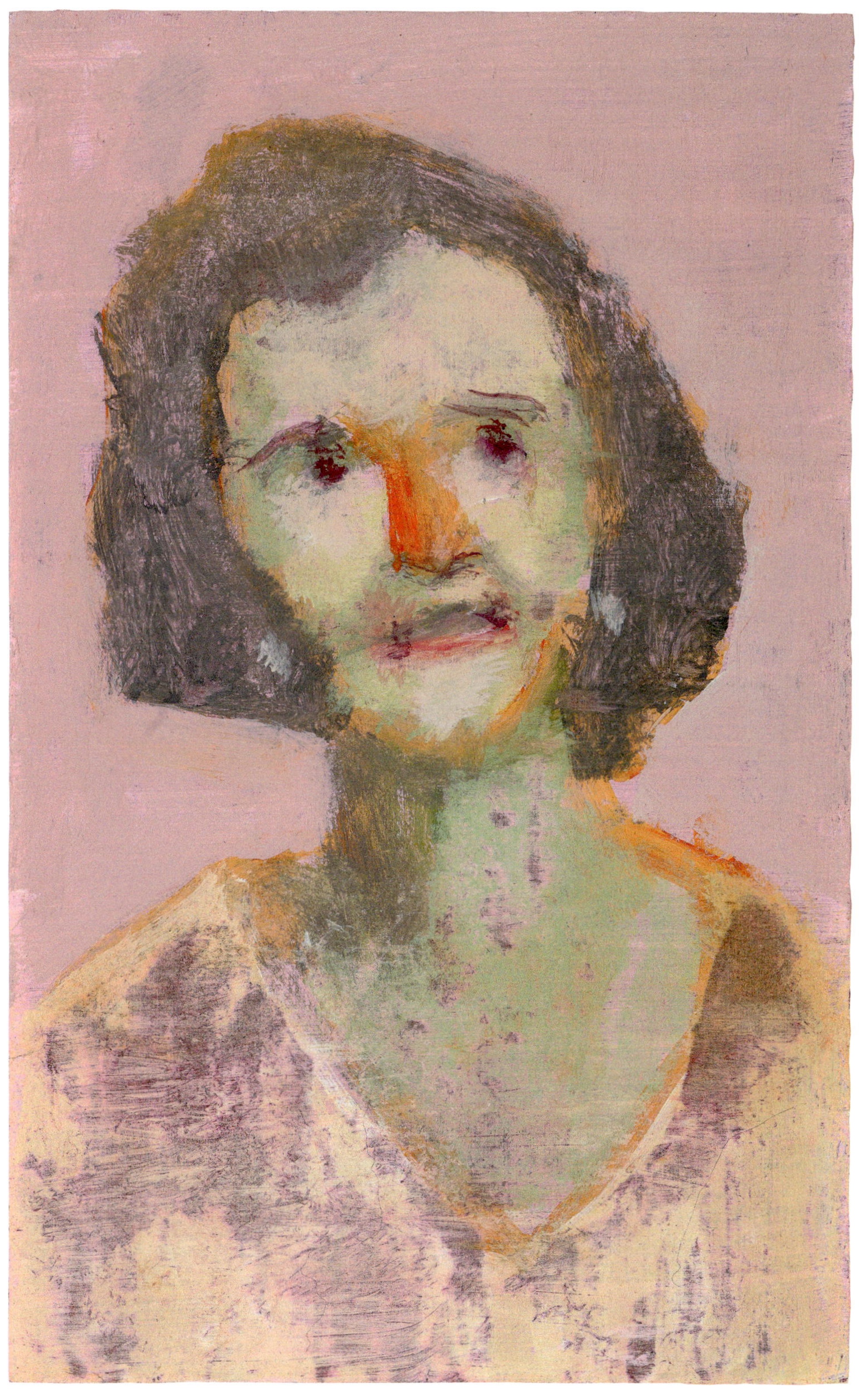

Heavens!, 2023

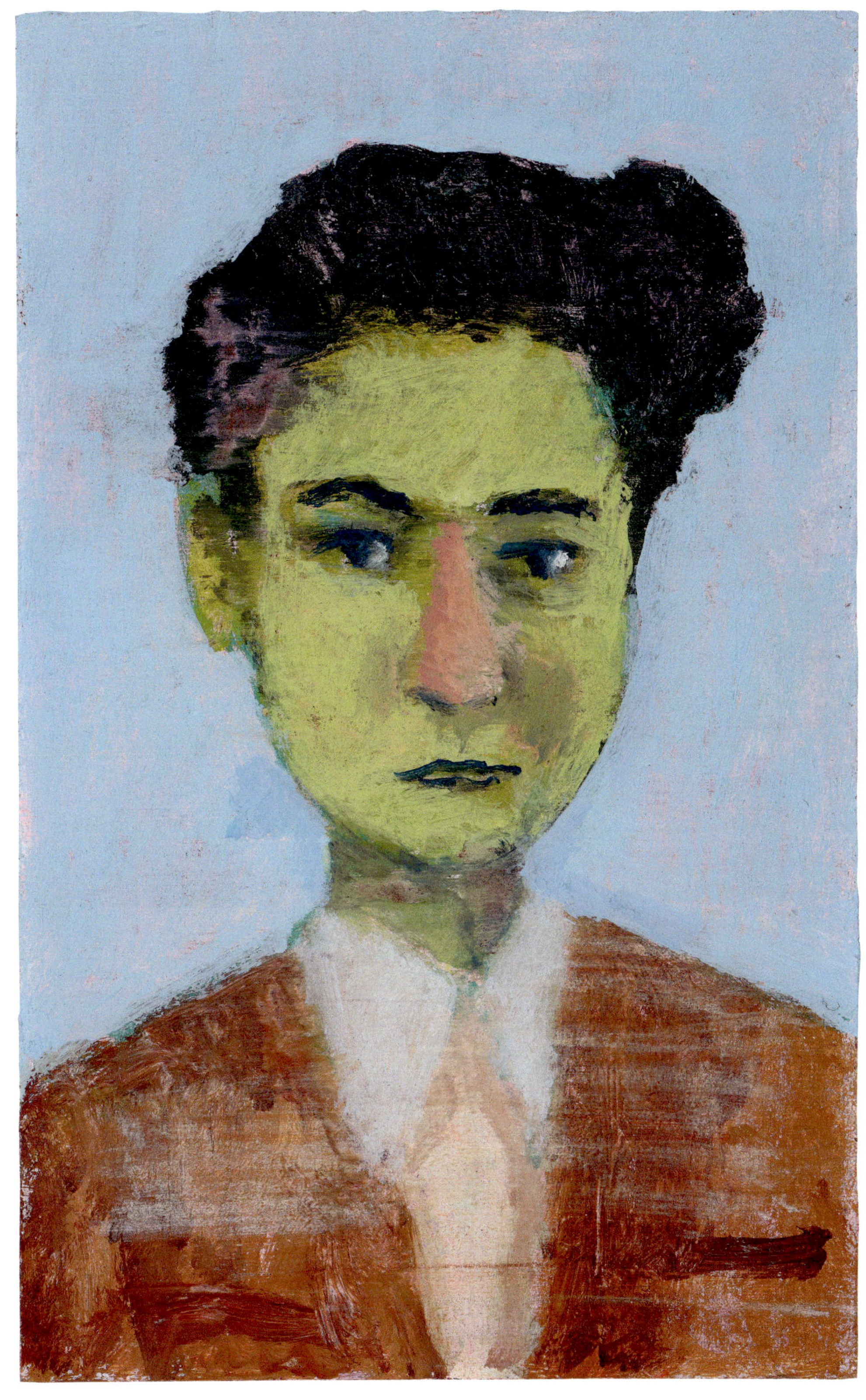

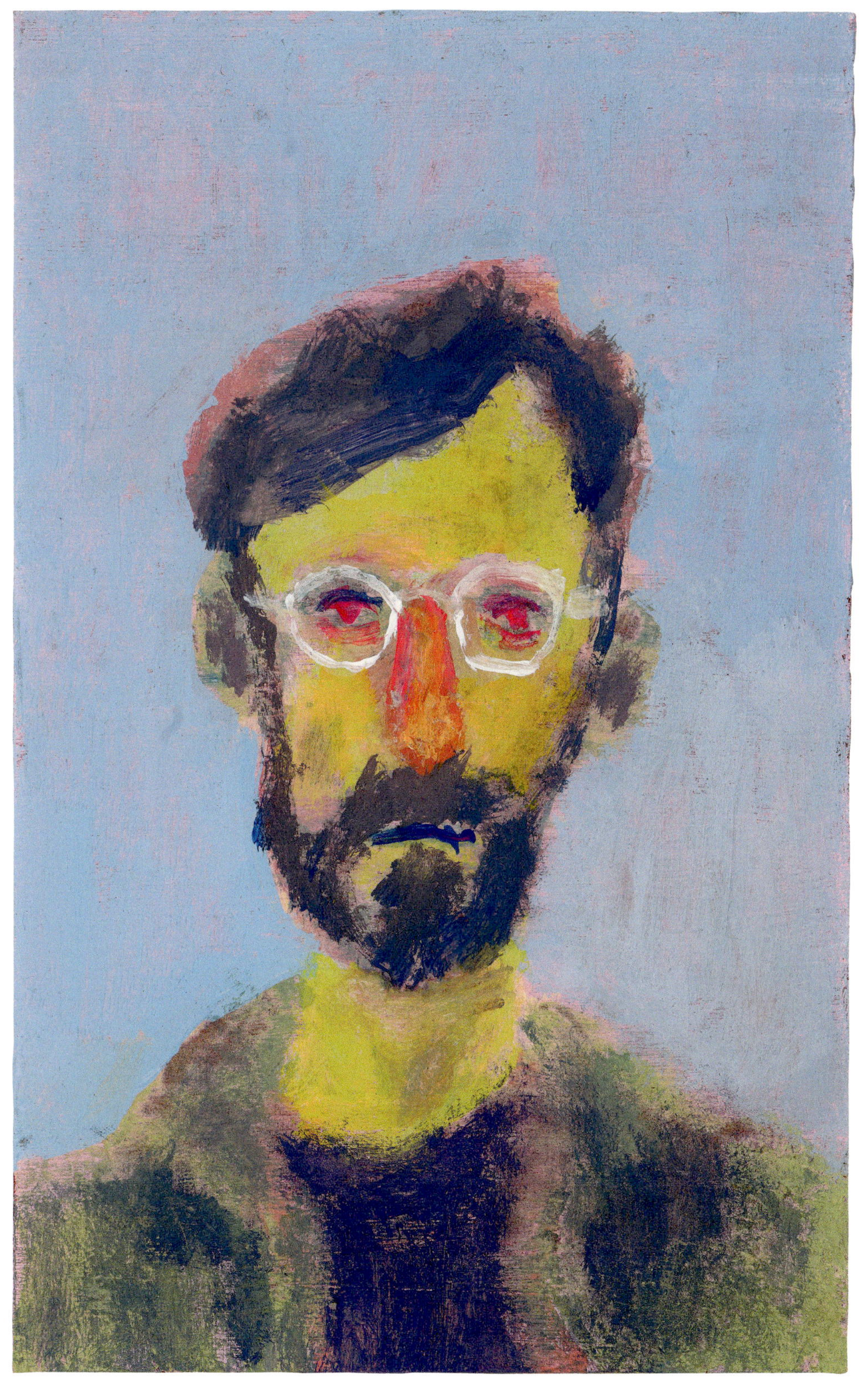

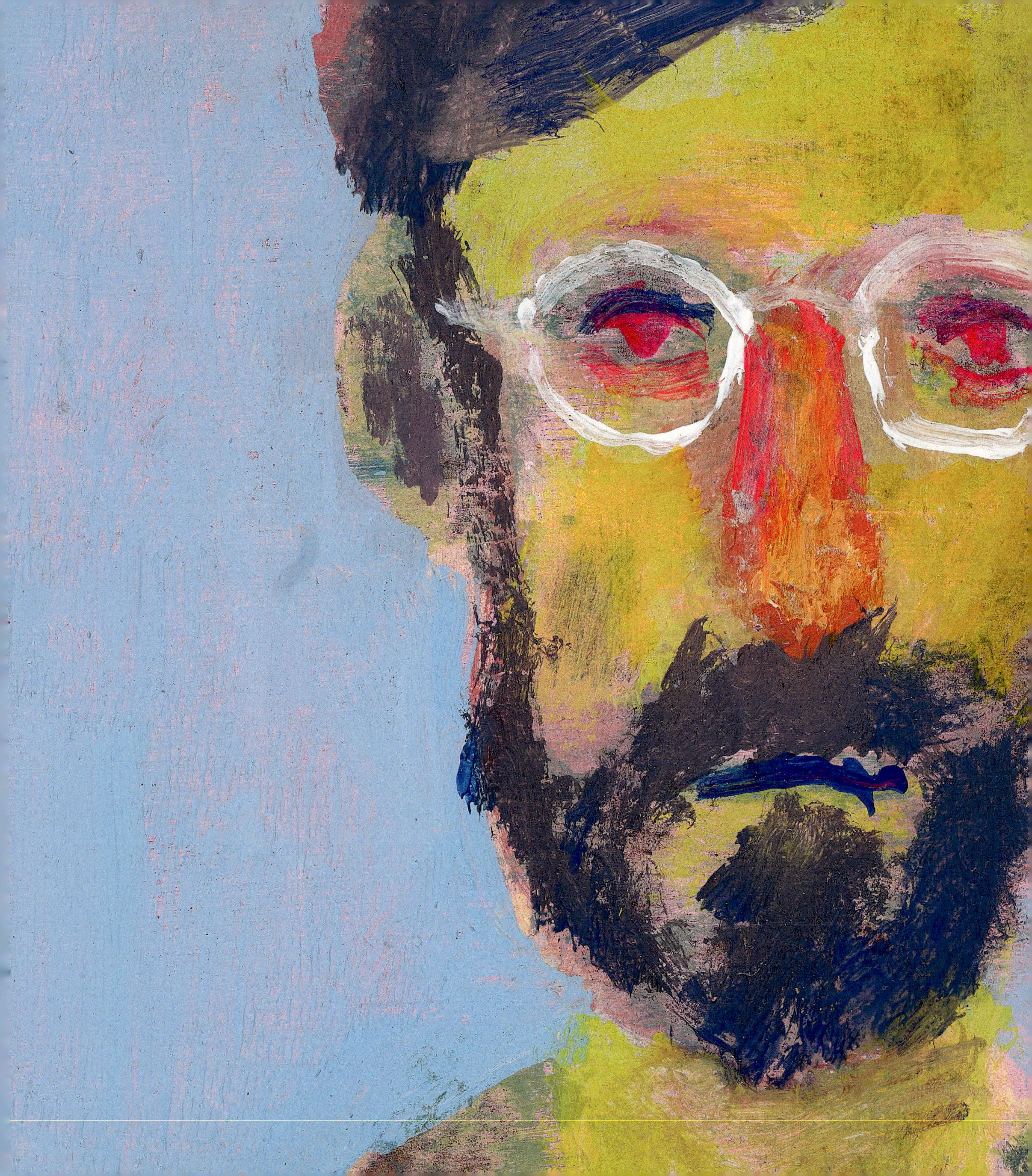

Jeesus!, 2023 (detail)

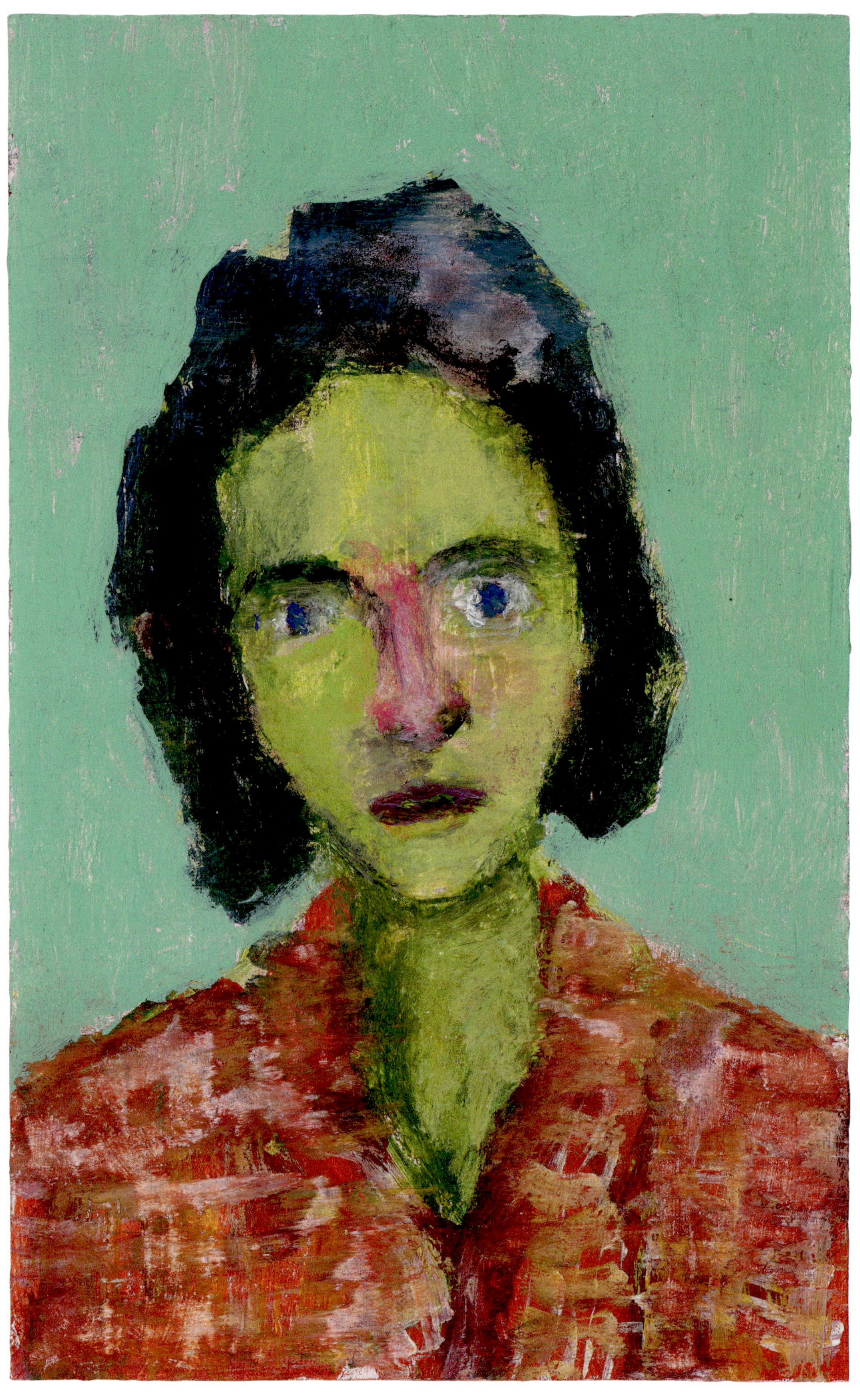

Knock Knock!, 2023

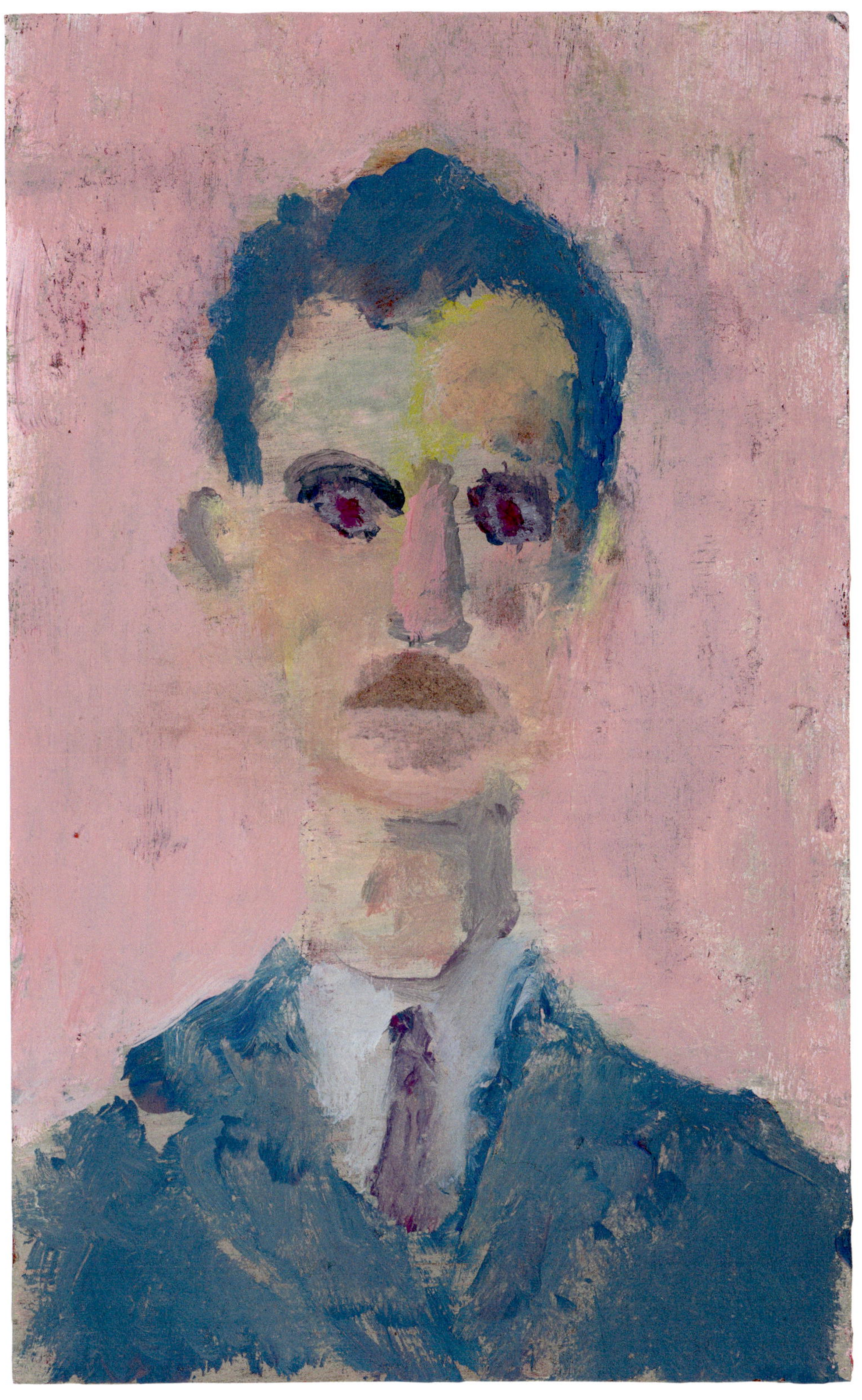

Likewise!, 2023

Magnificent!, 2023

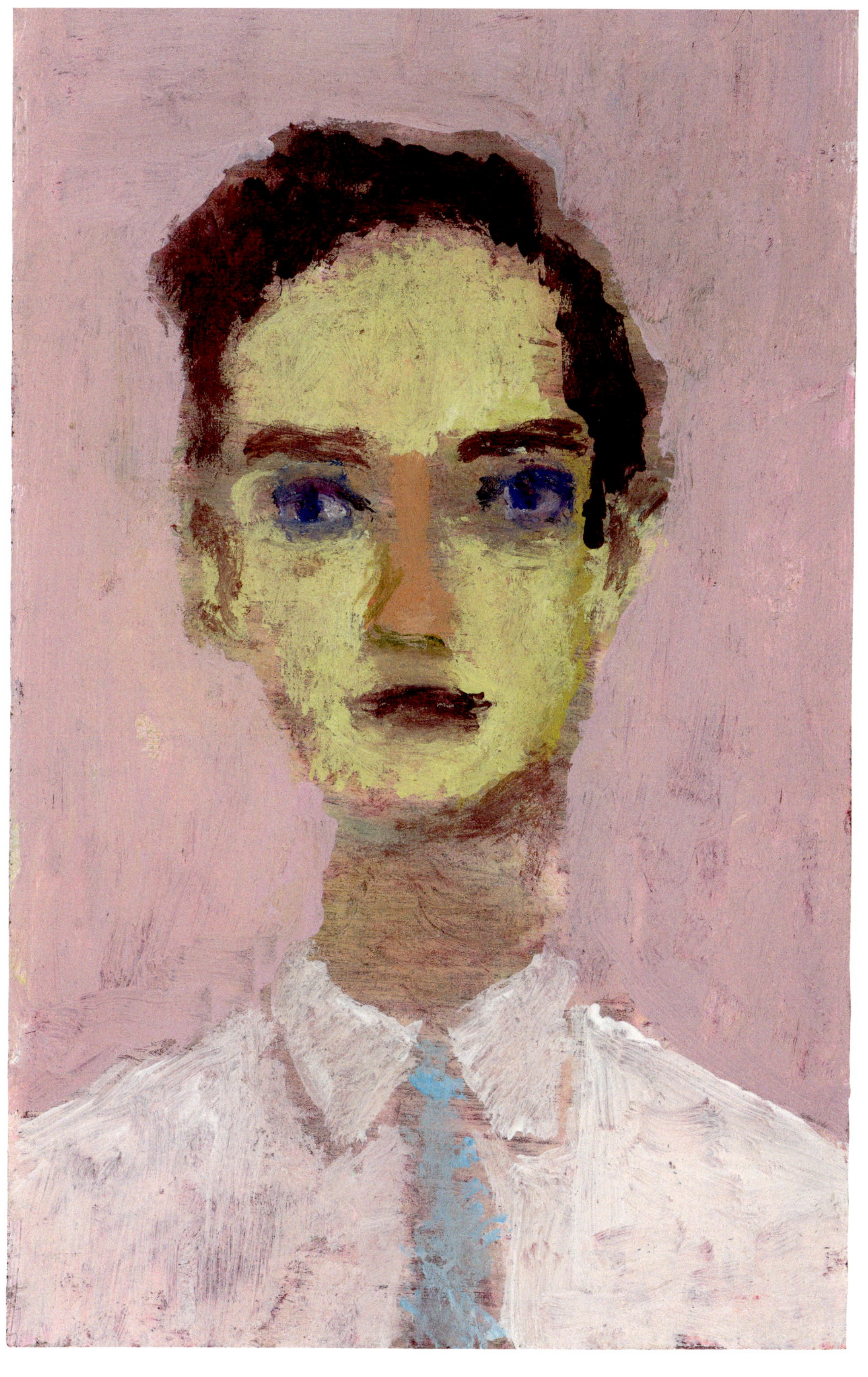

Never!, 2023

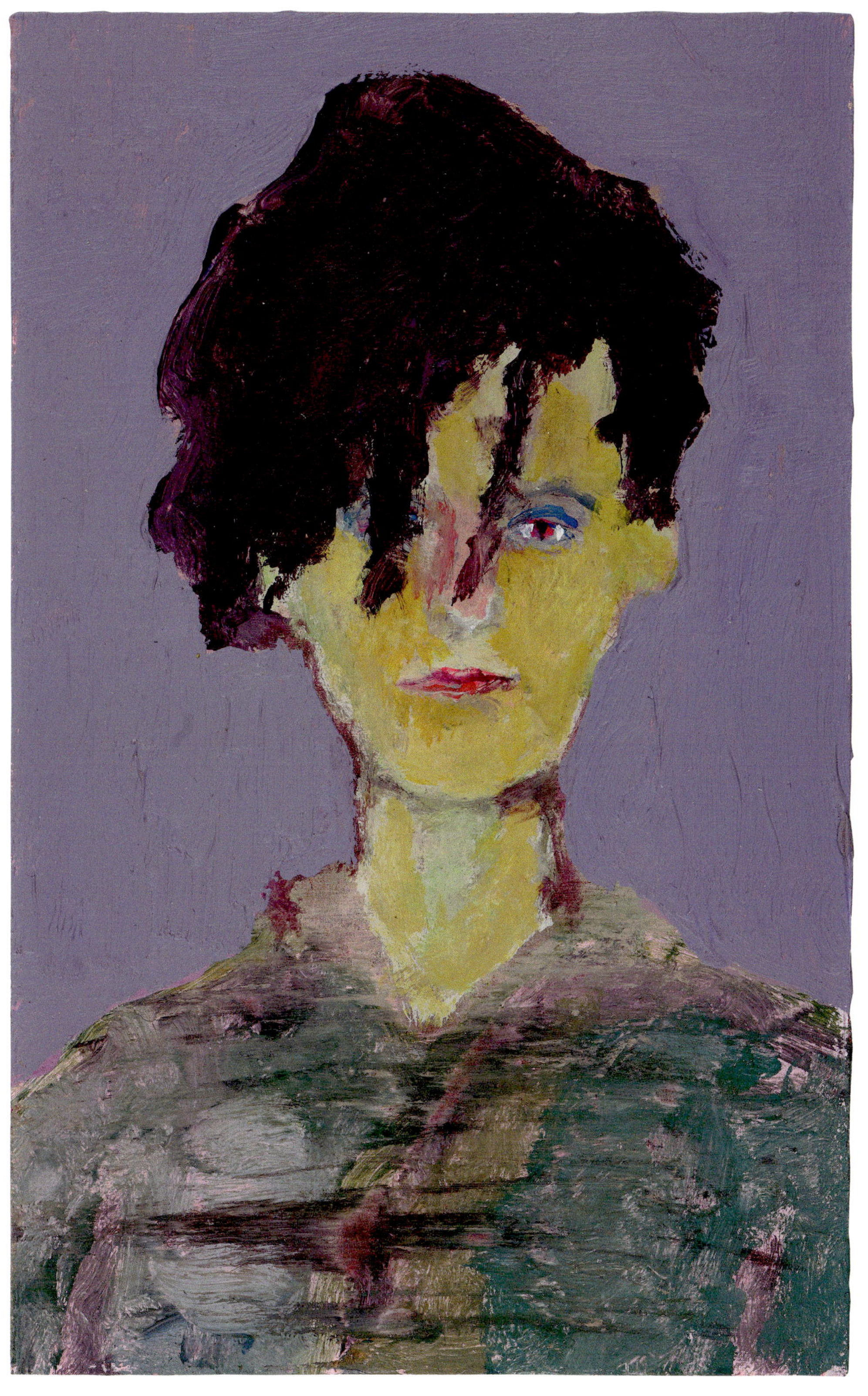

Never!, 2023 (detail)

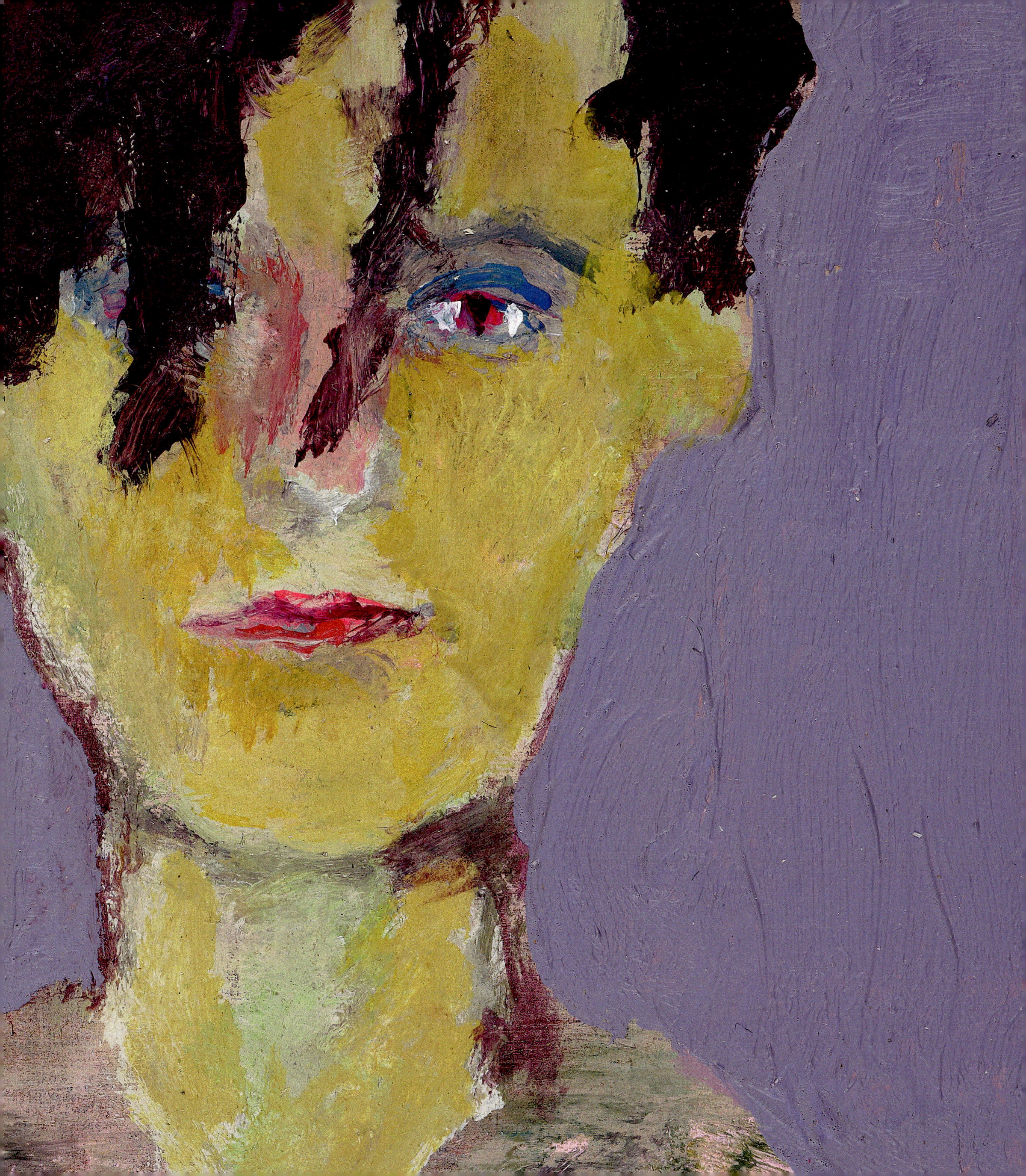

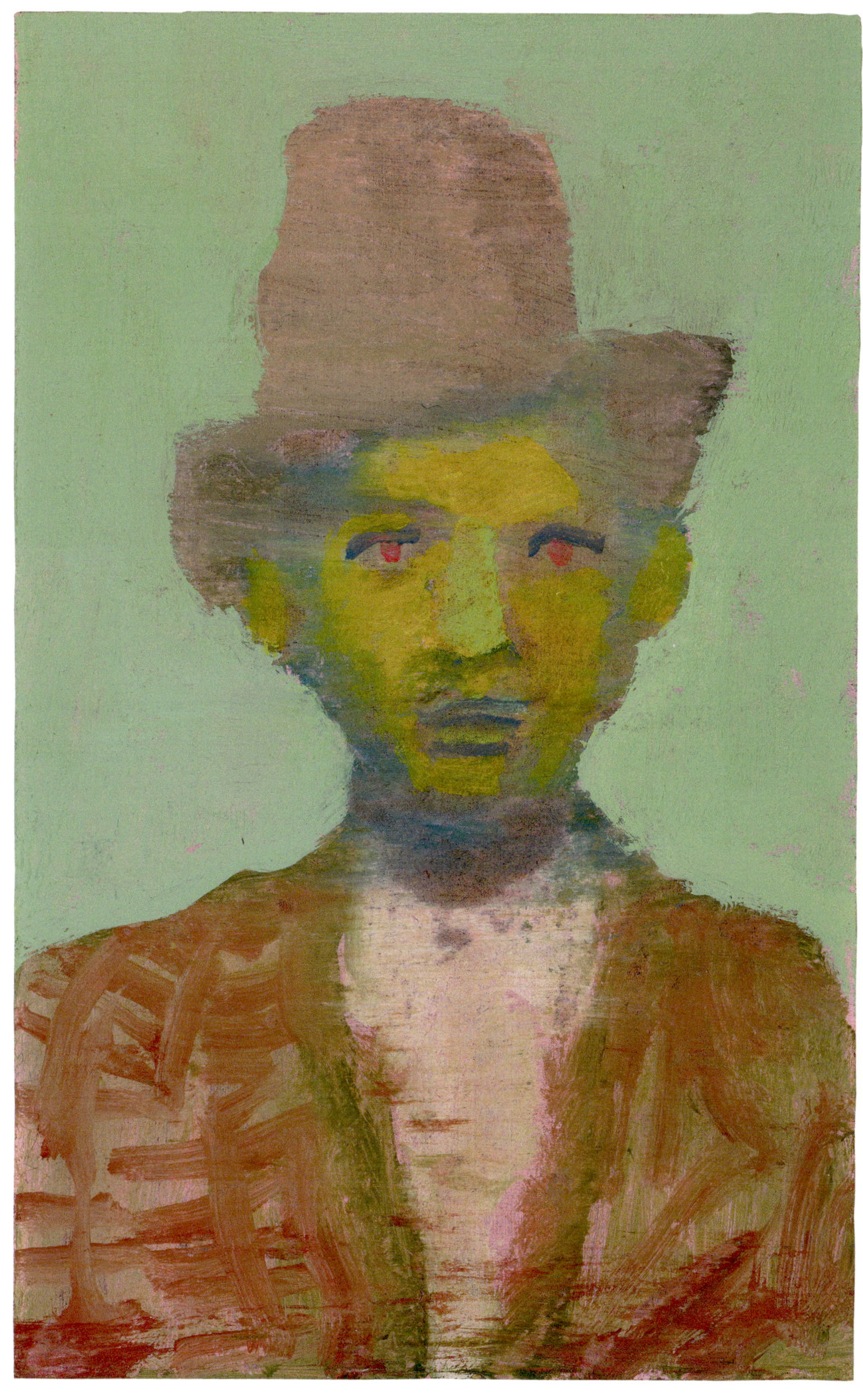

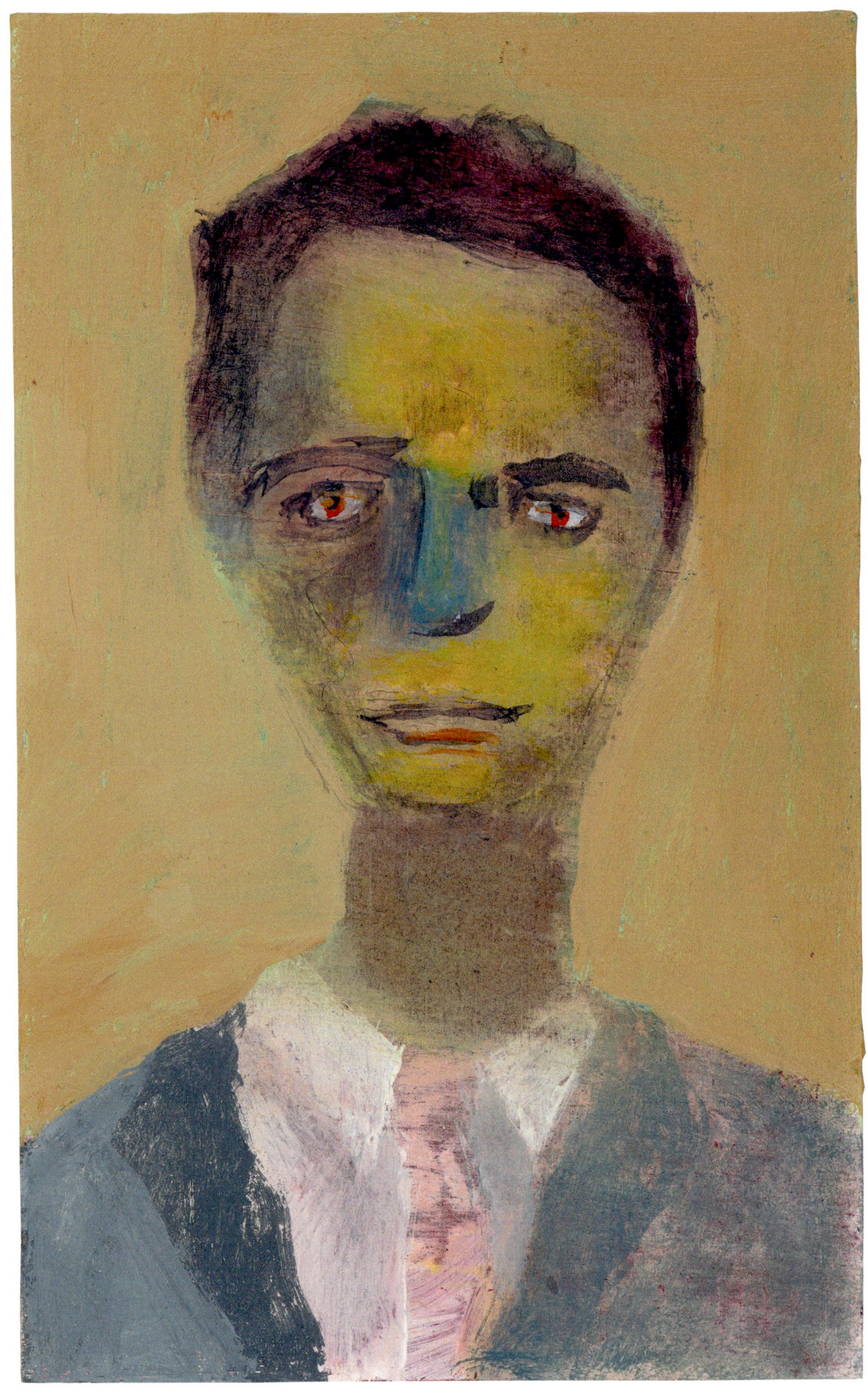

Please!, 2023

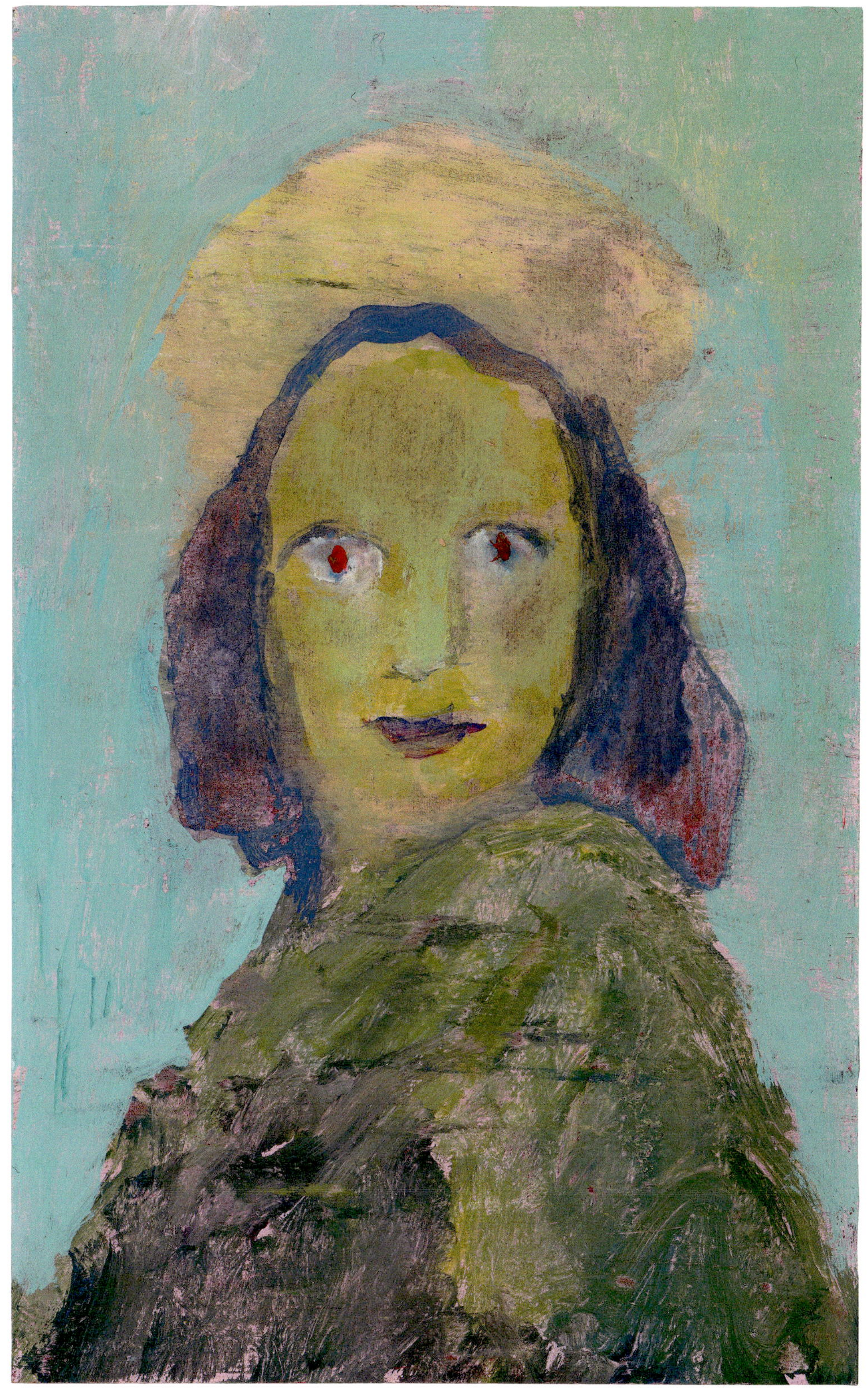

Quite!, 2023

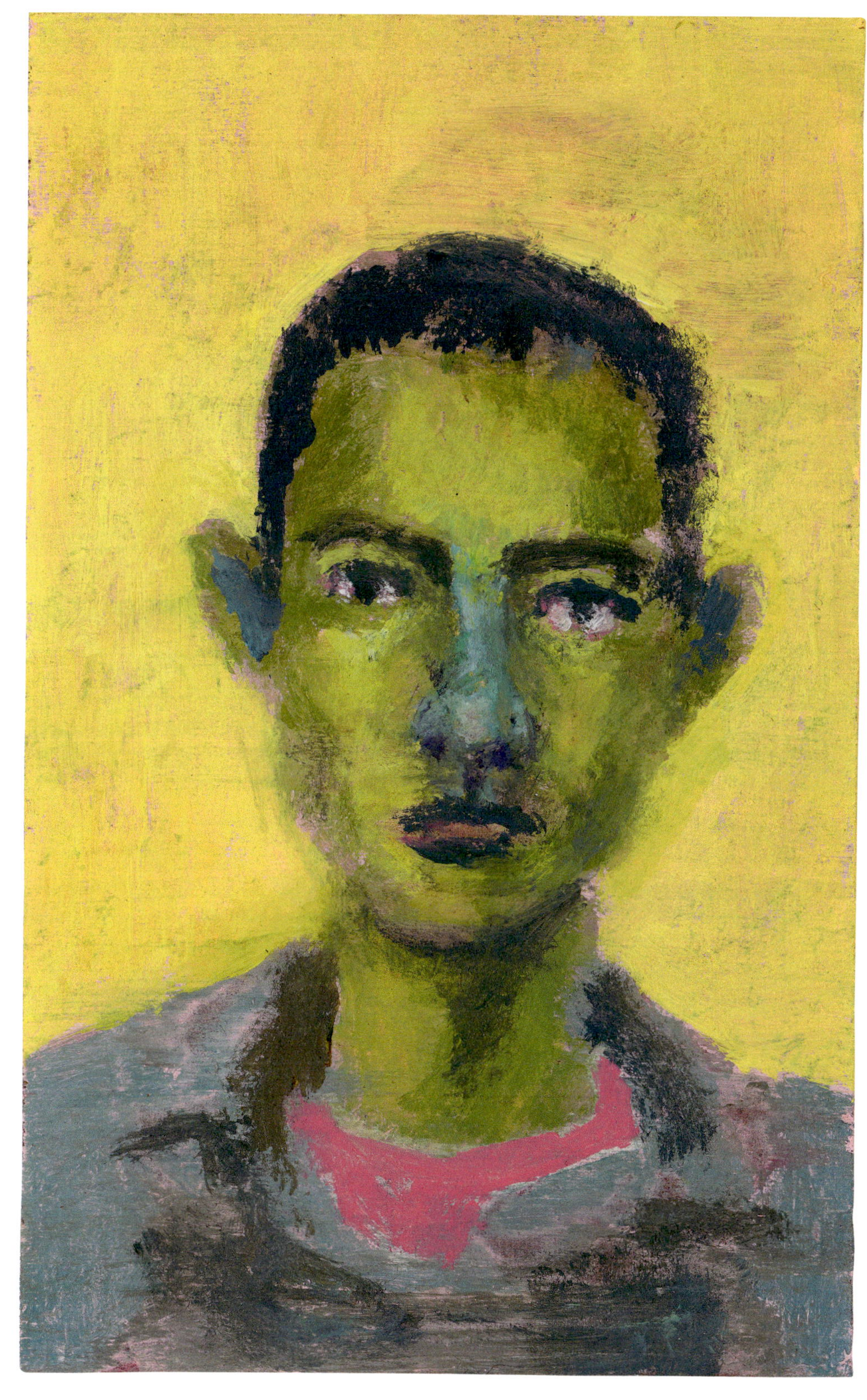

Rarely!, 2023 (detail)

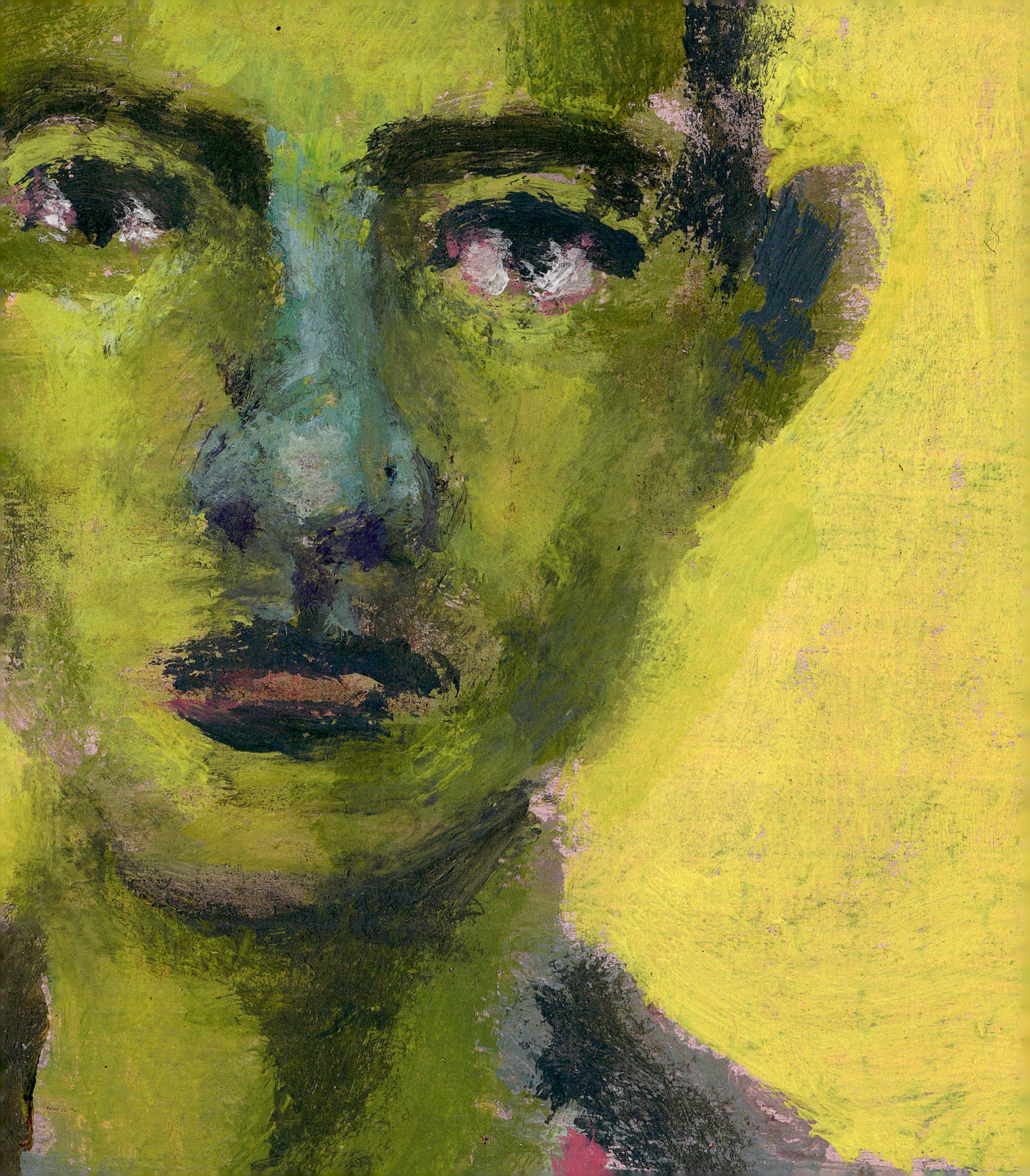

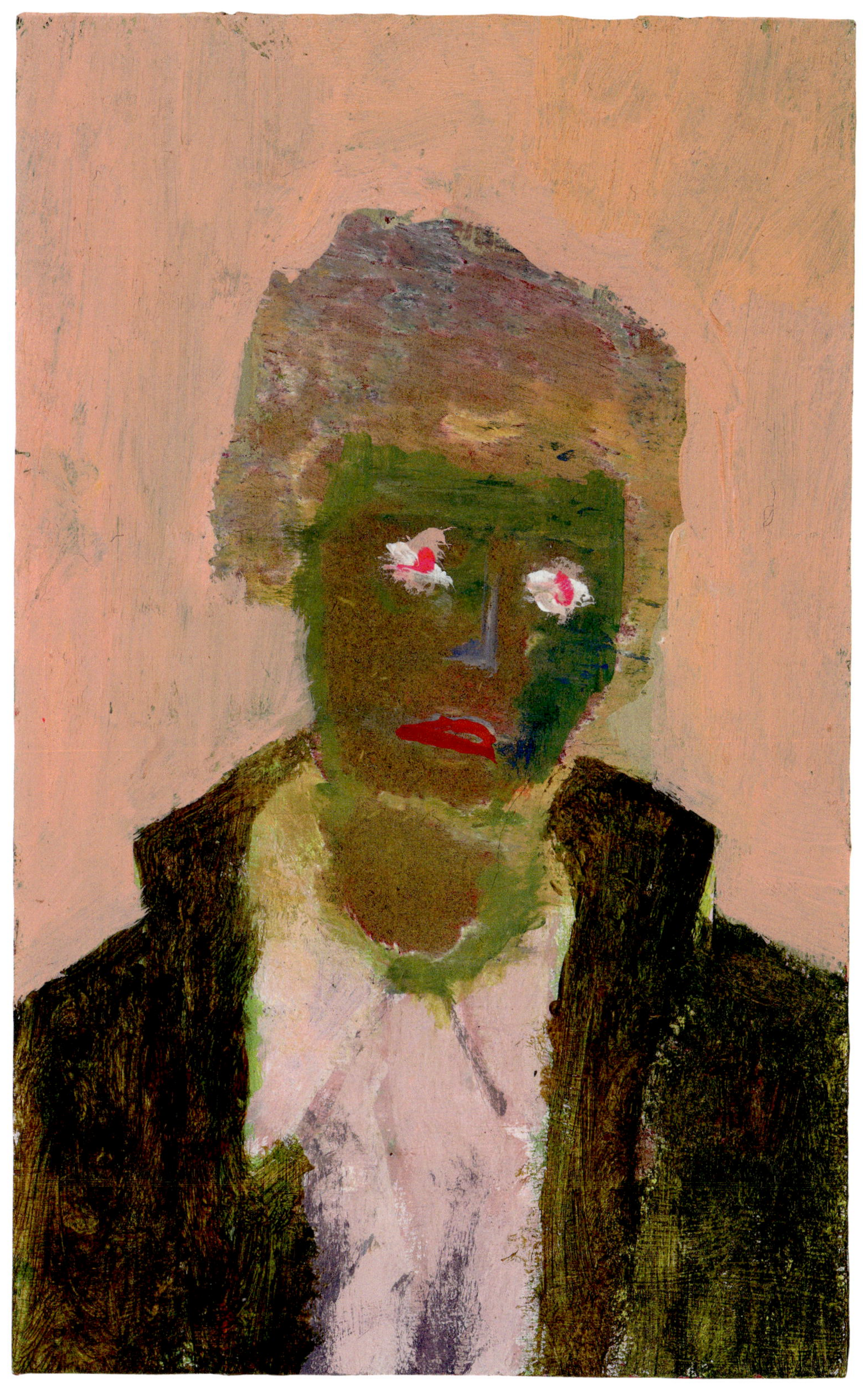

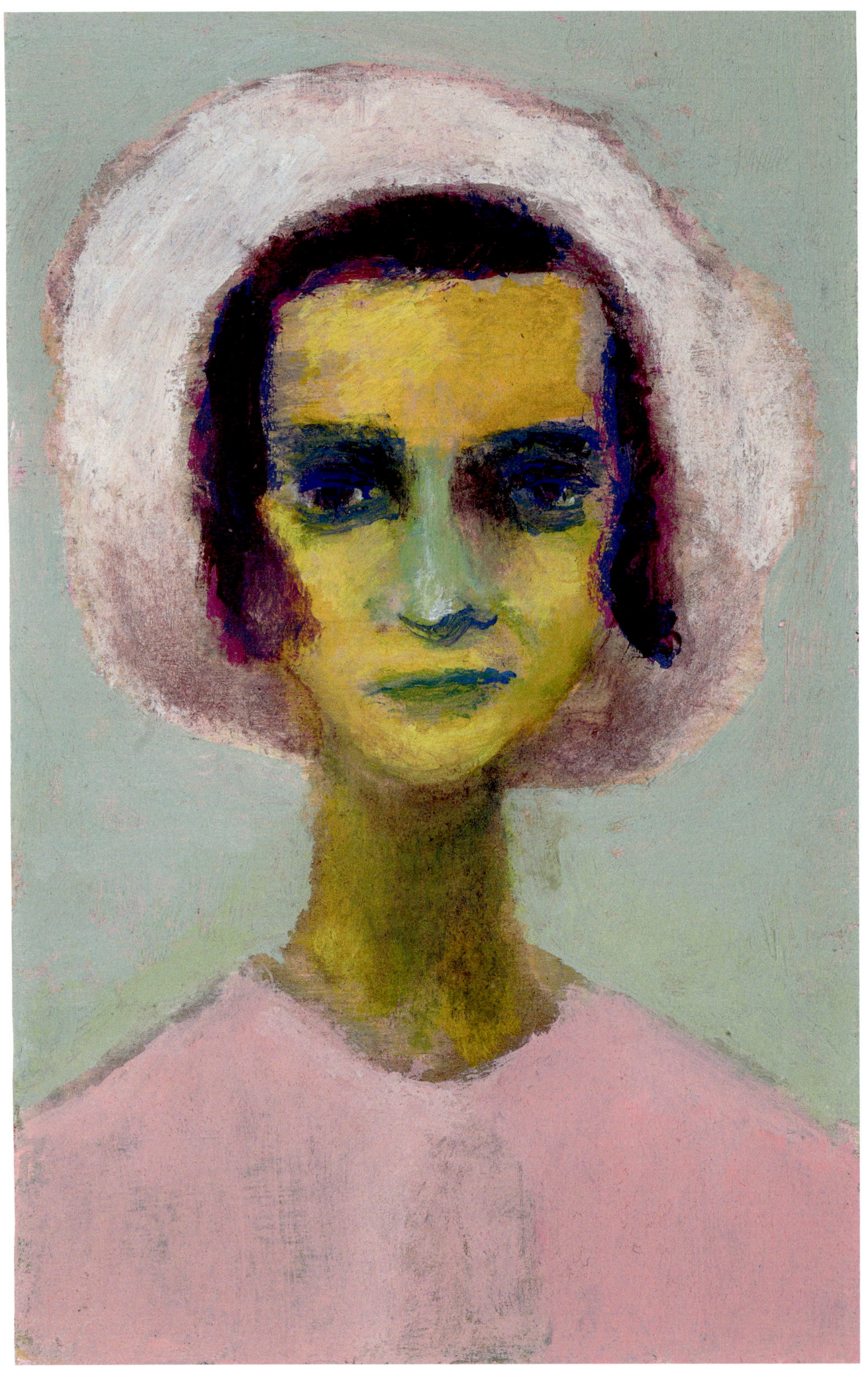

Tip Top!, 2023

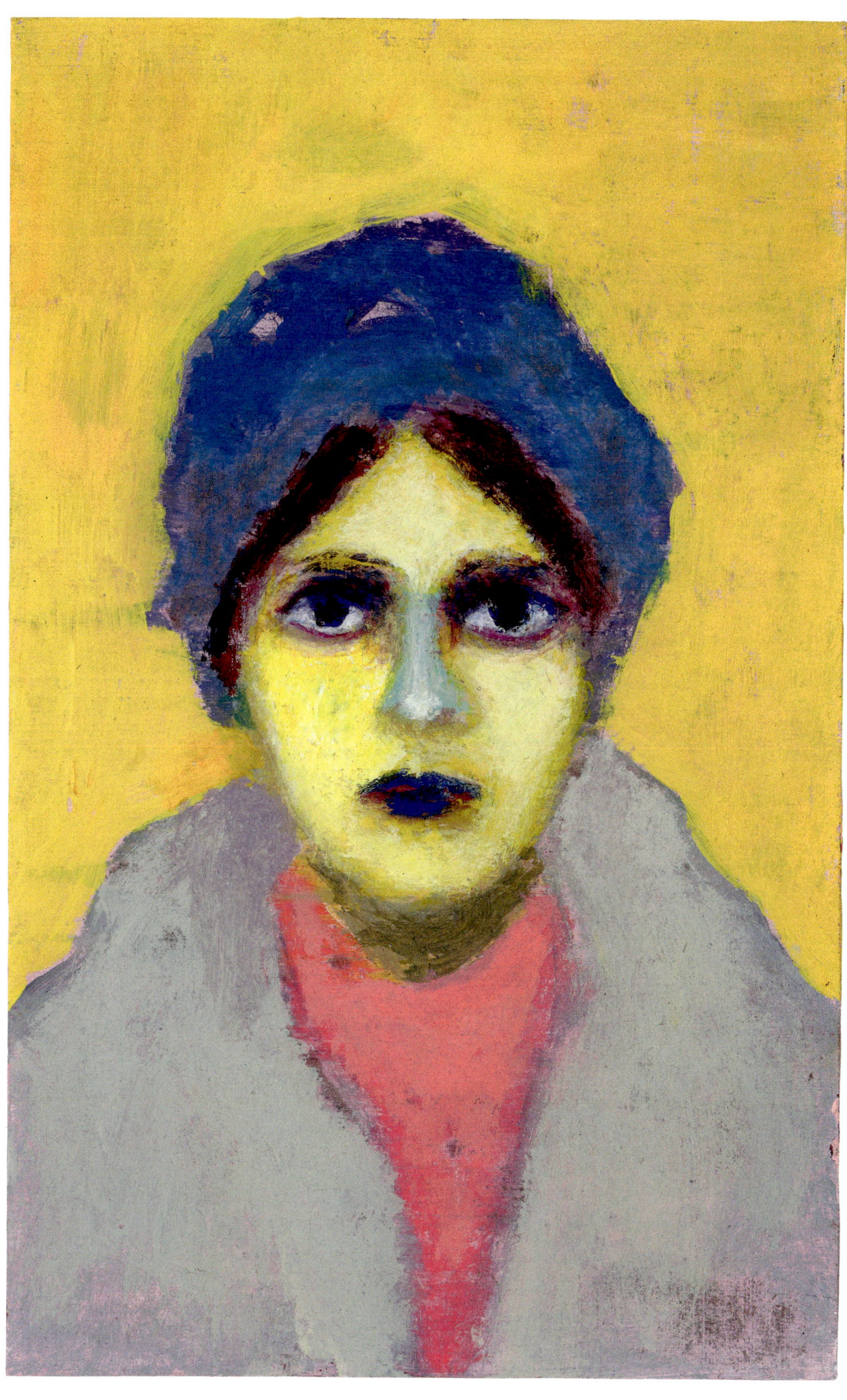

Unbelievable!, 2023

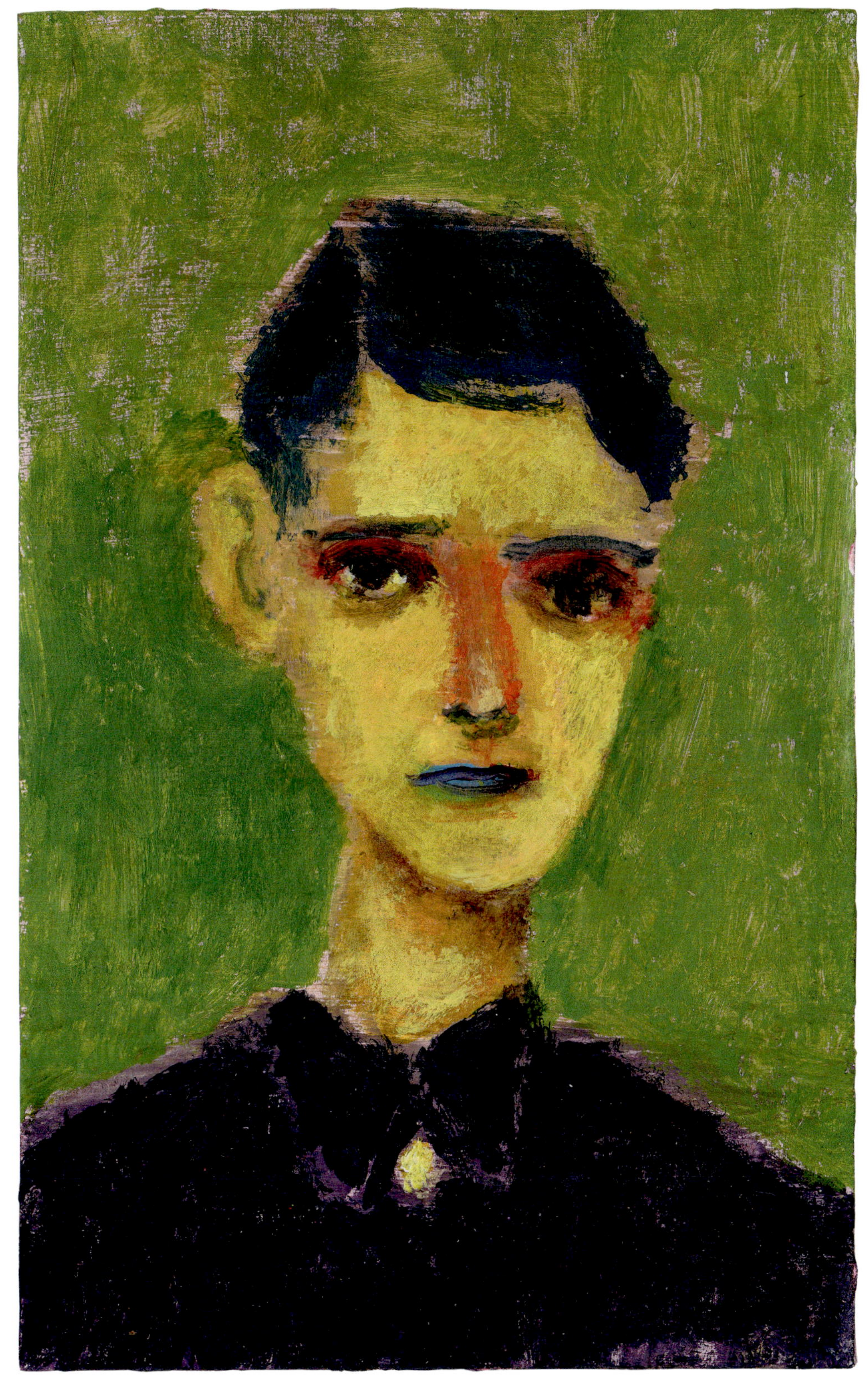

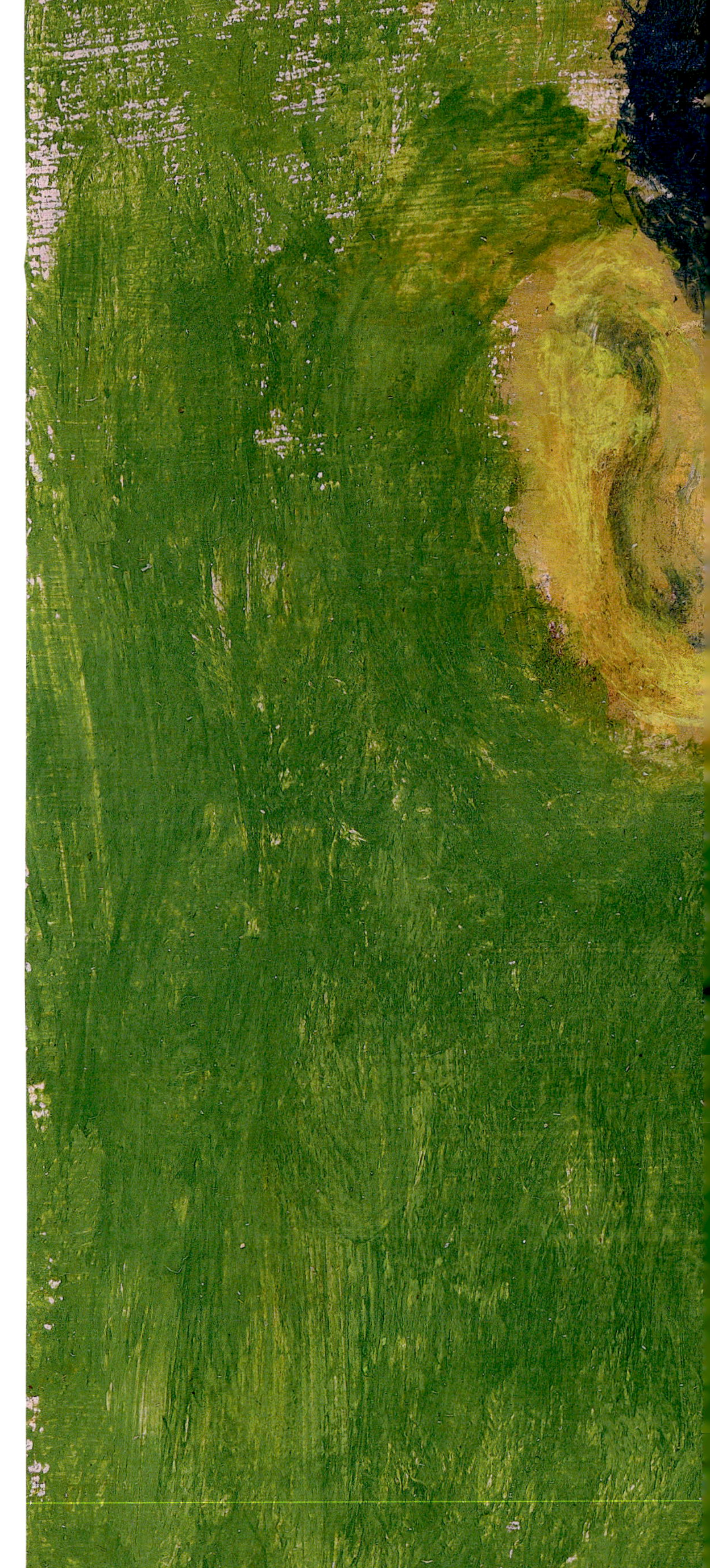

Very!, 2023 (detail)

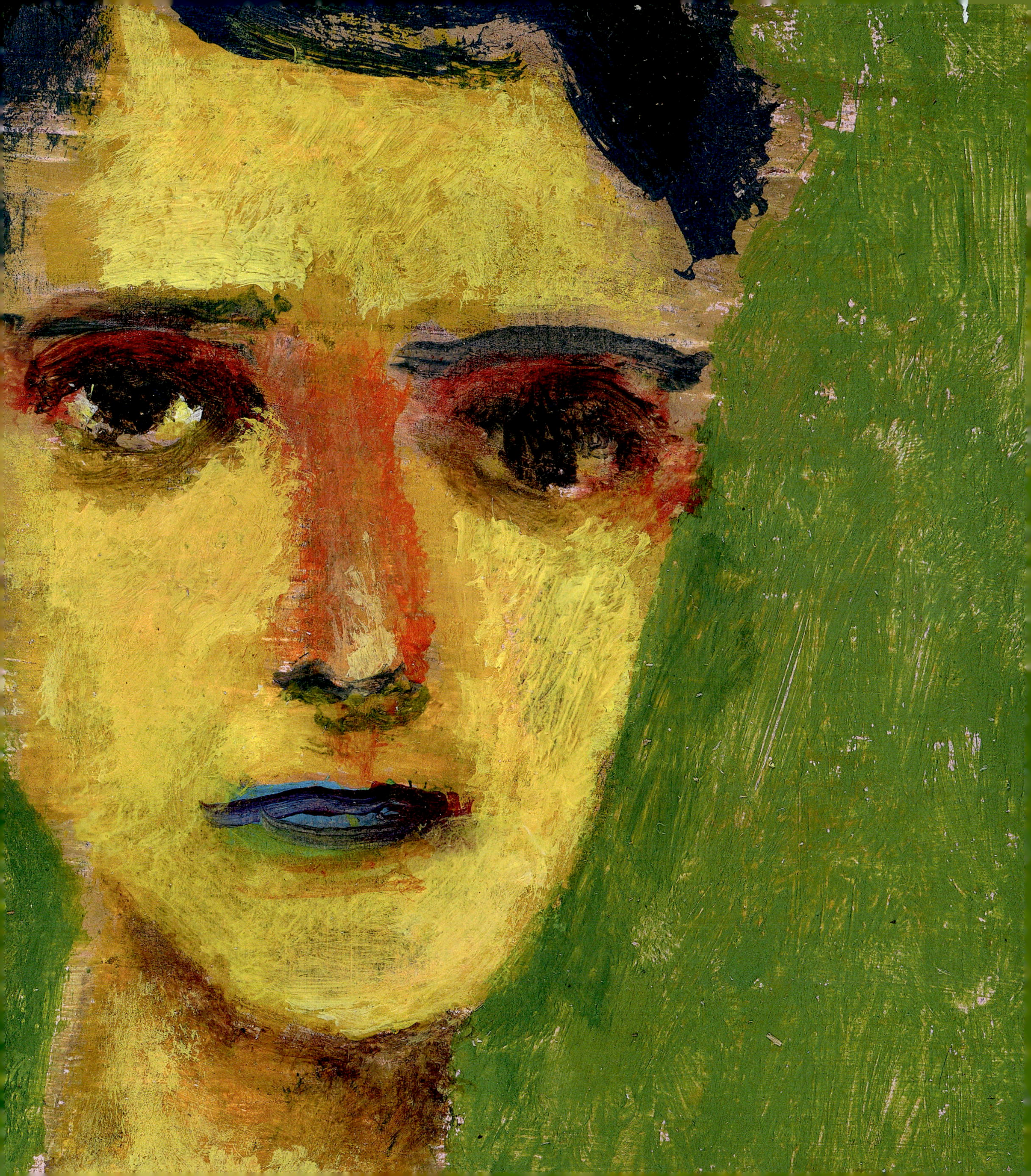

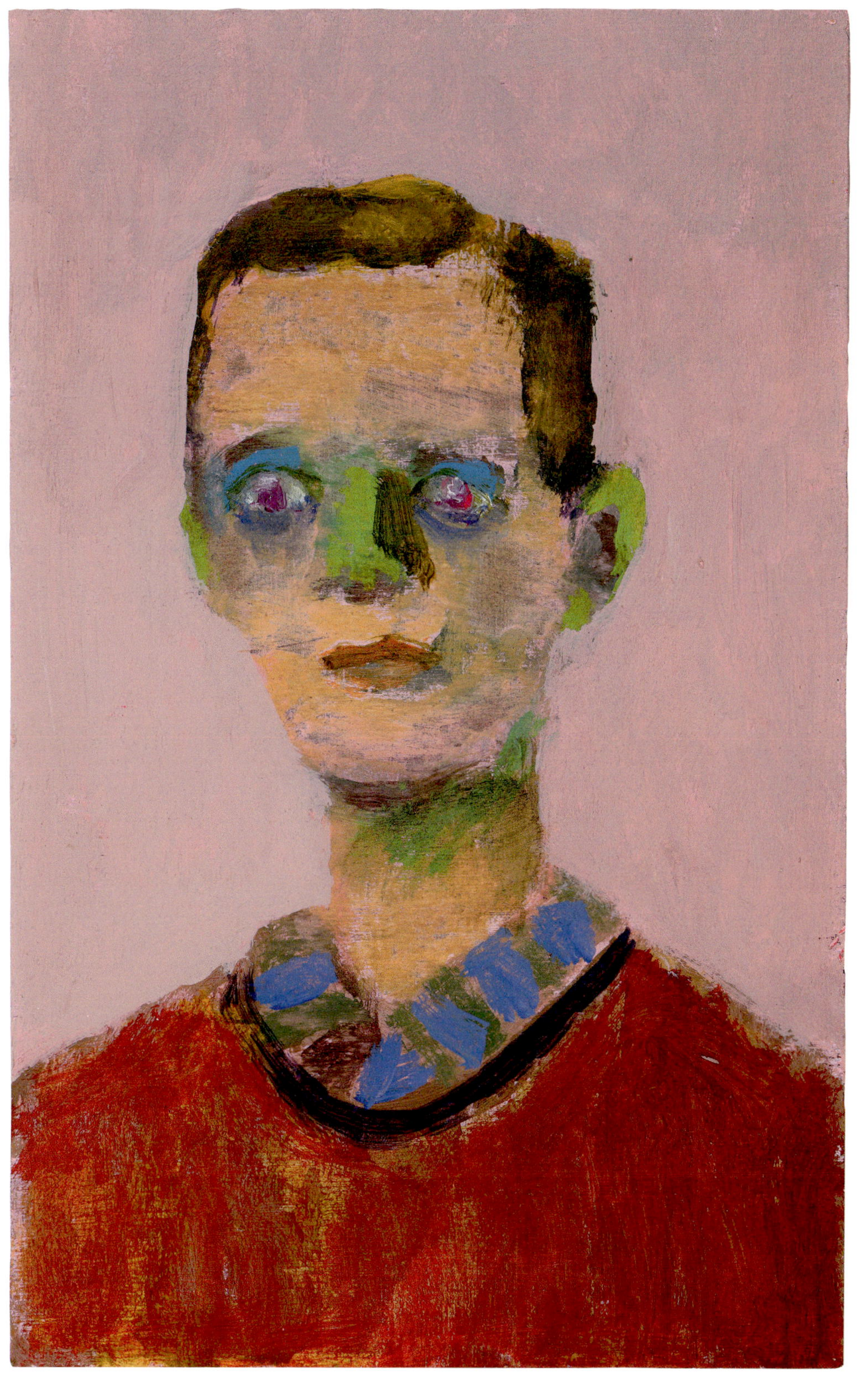

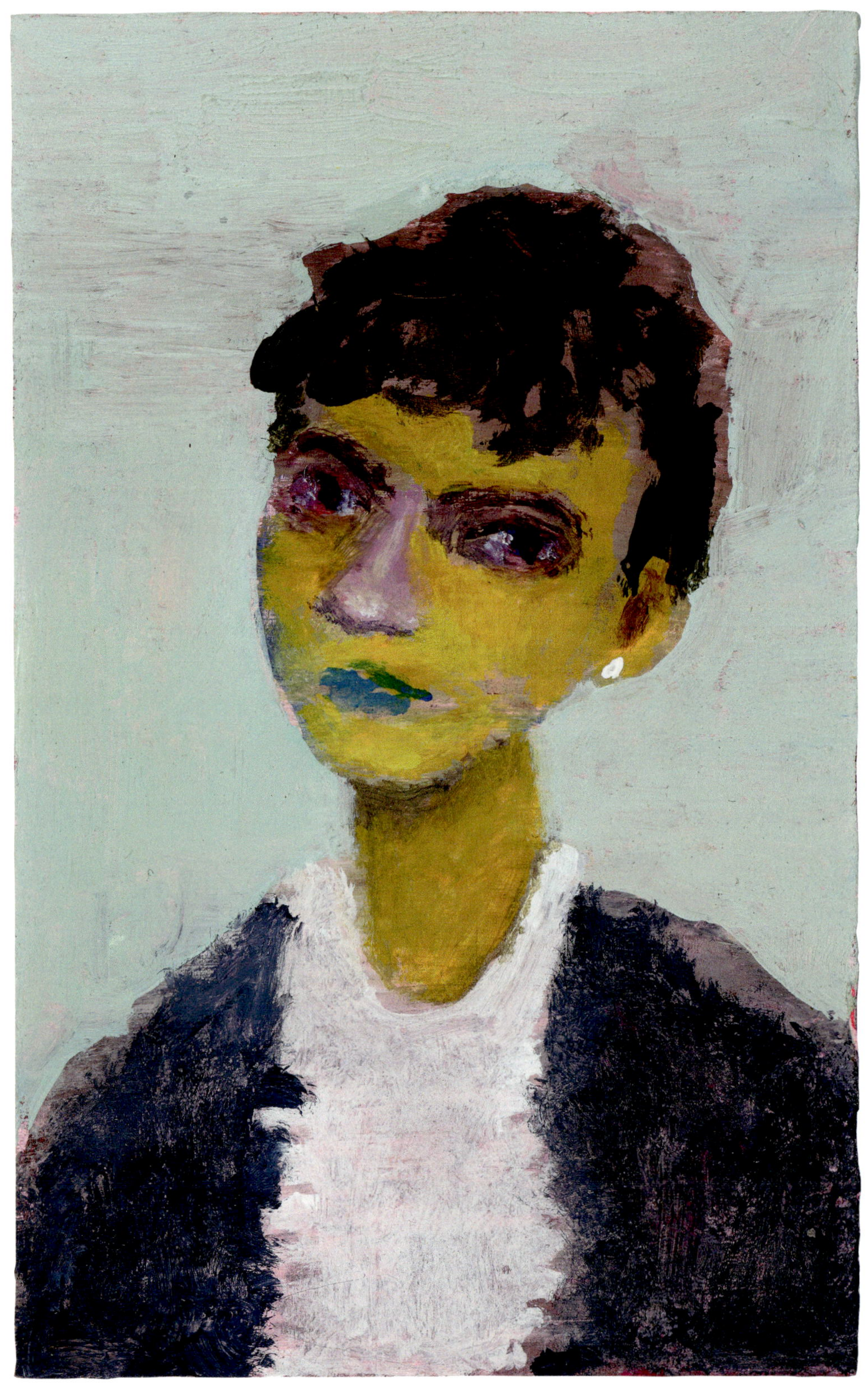

Xennial!, 2023

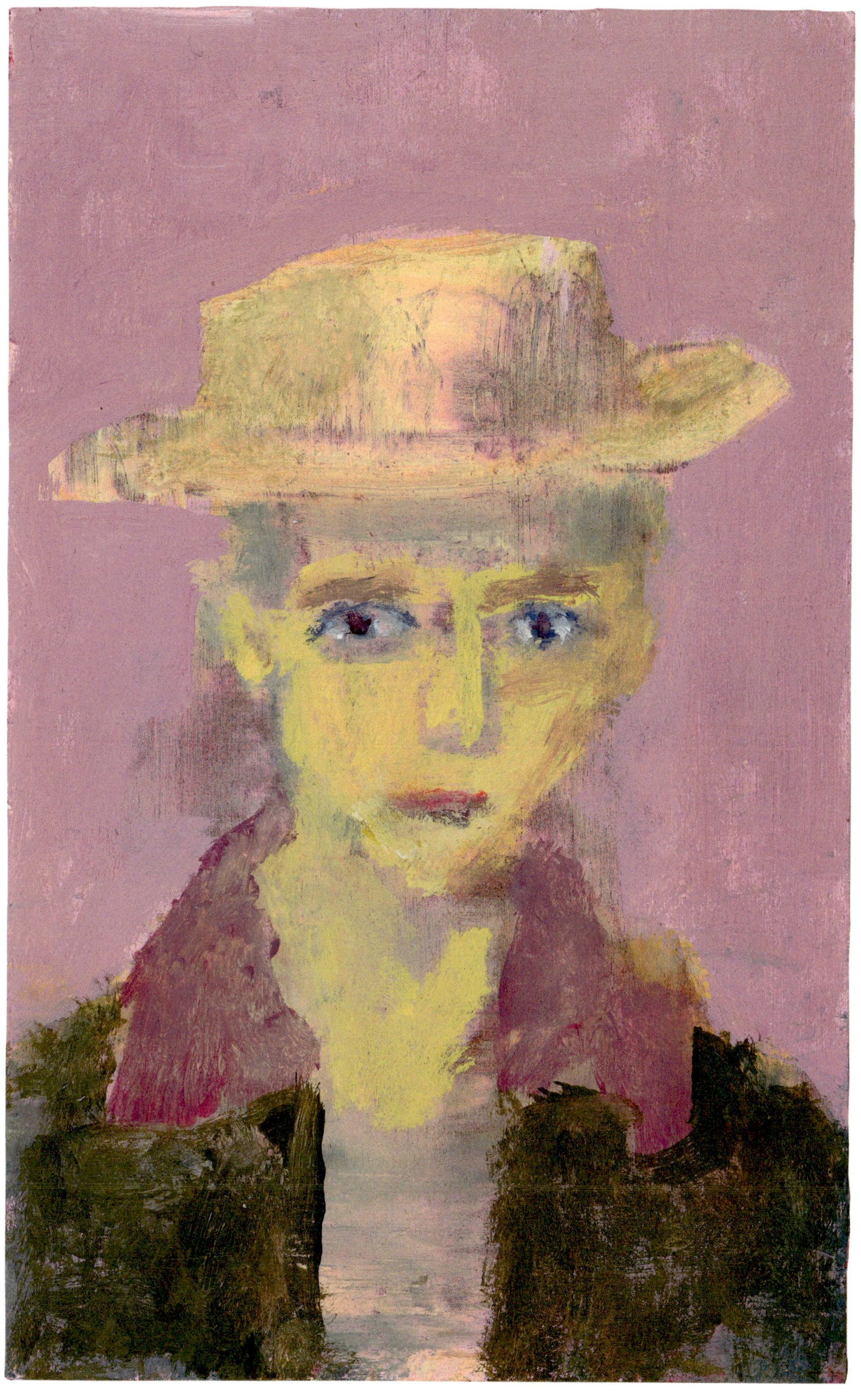

Yeehaw!, 2023

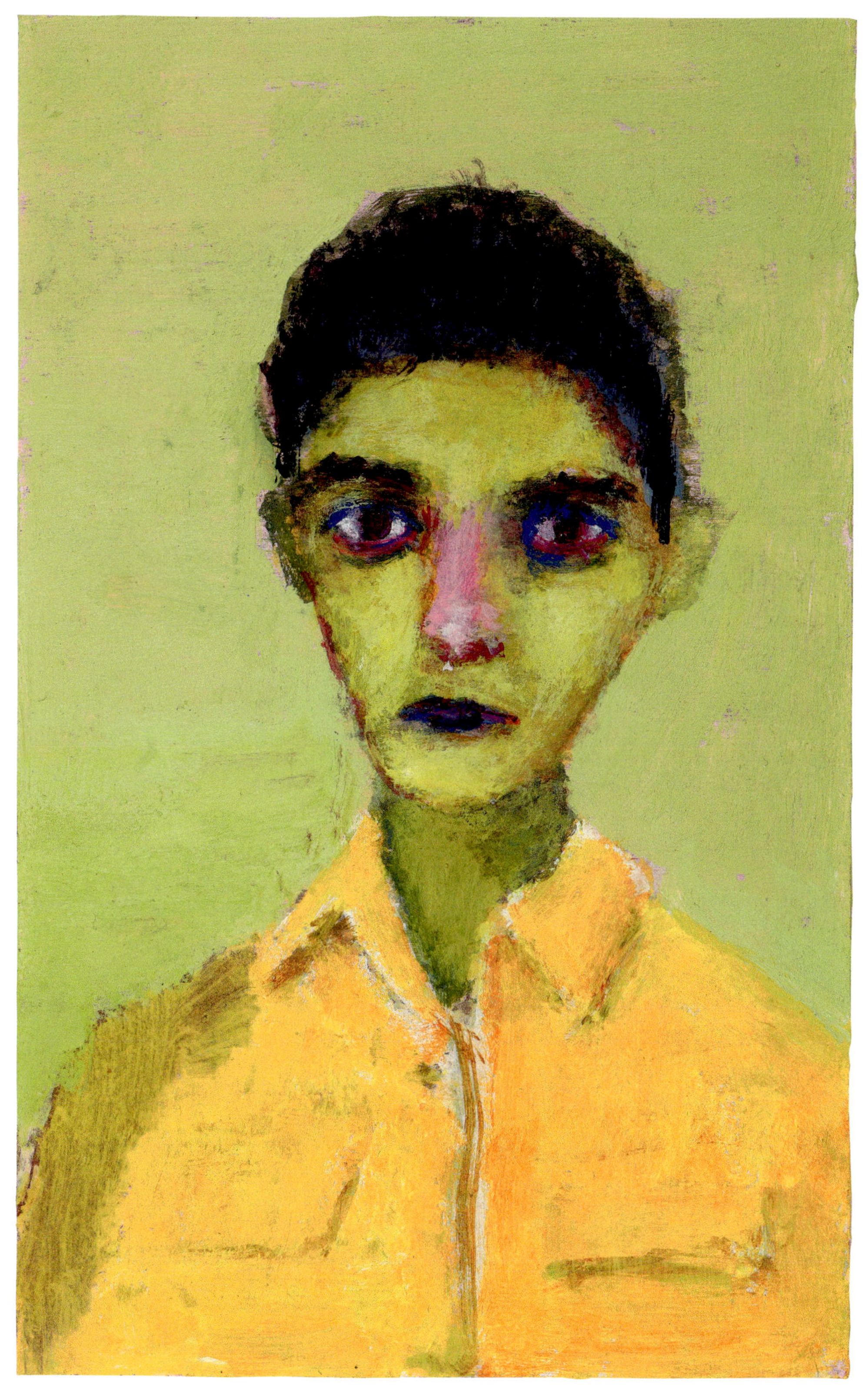

Ceri Hand: How long have you been painting?

Ben Sadler: There was a story my mum always used to tell, that I just wouldn't paint as a kid. By the time I reached the age of five, she was starting to get quite worried. She was a teacher. She asked me time and again why I didn't want to paint, and finally I told her, 'I can't make it look how I want it to look.' Around that time I had to do a drawing at school and because of that I ended up getting quite into drawing. But I still couldn't make paint go the way I wanted it to, so I still wouldn't paint. And then I remember trying some watercolours when I was a little older. Or, again, having to. There's something about *having* to do it, I think, and I remember being fascinated by how the colours mixed. I still couldn't paint things as I saw them, but I could make colours I liked. Then in my teenage years I got heavily into Warhammer and Dungeons & Dragons. I know it's quite a nerdy starting point, but painting these miniatures and their backgrounds taught me quite a lot about using acrylic paint. A few years later, when I'd opted to do A-level art, my dad bought me an oil-painting set and some boards as a surprise Christmas present. I was staying at his for a few days over Christmas, and he and my stepmum wanted to watch a film together, so he said, 'How about you go upstairs and do a painting of this pepper and this potato for me?' So again, I was forced into making. It was the first oil painting I'd ever made but there was something about it I liked. I didn't really know anyone who painted apart from my dad's sister, my Auntie Joan. There was one of her paintings in my nan's house of a green bottle and some oranges, and it used to fascinate me. And as I was painting the pepper, I realised I was trying to ape the green bottle that she had painted.

CH: What do you think it was about the still life that you were so drawn to?

BS: Painting always seemed quite distant in a way; we never went to art galleries but it was that connection to my auntie, knowing that she painted this thing and that there was a view that I recognised from my gran and grandad's house in the background. It made it all quite tangible, I think. And then I became really obsessed with painting during my A levels and spent a very intense two years making ever larger paintings because I thought that I needed to go bigger. My mum was really accommodating. It was just the two of us rattling around in the house, so I asked her if I could use our spare bedroom as a painting studio, and she said yes. There was an old sofa bed in there, and I took everything else out of the room and used to find large bits of paper that I could put up to make these massive paintings that I then used to take into school. My art teacher was really accommodating too. She'd say, 'What do want to make a painting about?' And I'd always say, 'A self-portrait where I look angry.' That was pretty much what I wanted to do. And then I went to art college. There was a lot more space at art college, so I got into sculpture; I found out a lot more about art and artists and drifted away from painting for quite a while and then started working with my friend Phil Duckworth as Juneau Projects. We were doing a lot of performance work and installation, and then painting gradually started creeping back into that. Eventually, when my wife Katy and I had Hazel – our daughter – that changed things. I was doing a lot of music before we had Hazel, but I couldn't really do that so much at that time.

I spent two years after she was born just being tired, and painting seemed to be something I could do in the evenings that was not a counterpoint, but in Juneau we were focusing more on public art projects and working with people. Painting fulfilled that missing part. And then for the last ten years I've pretty much made a painting every day. They have tended to be small. It's just become a part of my day now, making a painting.

CH: You use your home as your studio for painting. How does the domestic environment inform the work?

BS: It wasn't really practical using oil paints in the living room, so I decided to use acrylic instead. A lot of the painters I like use oil paints. I enjoy thinking about how I might get towards some of the textures they create, but with acrylics. I've always had the TV on in the background when I'm doing stuff. So I'm really used to drawing or painting with the TV on and a cat sitting next to me or on my lap. Oscar gets paint on his tail quite a lot! So yeah, the house becomes part of the work.

CH: I'm curious as to whether family life or the context of your home gets infused into the painting process.

BS: Yes, definitely. There are a lot of paintings of Hazel, for example. From where I sit, she'll be on the sofa opposite and I'll just paint her while she's playing her Nintendo Switch. So that definitely comes in. Our cat Oscar's always around. He's normally really good at striking a pose and holding it, so you can get a good ten to twenty minutes to get that painted in. I do try and paint Katy, but she's quite a tough critic so I have to be careful painting her! And then there's lots of things that creep in, like plants in the living room, or, especially when Hazel was younger, little objects that she'd made or her toys. She likes animals a lot, so there's always a horse or a bear or a fox somewhere in the field of view. It's like that bit in *The Usual Suspects* where he's just made up the story from all the things on the wall behind the police officer. It's pulling bits from around me, or if I need a plant in there it's quite often the same one that features in a lot of paintings just because that's the plant that's in front of me while I'm painting.

CH: Your painting practice has a calm, meditative quality, but it also sounds diaristic in a sense, that processing of the everyday. But the two series of paintings for this book – *Exclamations!* and *You and I* – seem to have a different focus. Could you walk us through how these series came about?

BS: Painting every day, I often make just one-off paintings, but then every so often I'll paint something and I'll think, 'I want to paint another one of these.' I think that is how the *Exclamations!* series began. I spent some time looking at archives of public-domain black and white photographs, and they were quite odd, strangely timeless. They're images from the early twentieth century, but a lot of the people in the photographs looked very now, very contemporary in that way so many fashions are reassimilated. I started making a painting of one of the people in it and the thought popped into my head while I was painting it that it resembled Paul Merton, and then the face sort of shifted in my mind from Paul Merton to this character being a curator of an exhibition. In my imaginary interaction with him, I'm trying to remember if we've met before, and he's trying to do the same, and that led me to think about art openings and the very specific feelings I have at these events. Looking at lots of photographs of different people chimed with that idea too – of coming into contact with quite a broad range of people. It's something that's always fascinated me about exhibition openings, that there's so many things going on. You're in an art gallery space, where you might have one way of acting, where you're looking quite objectively at the works that are on the wall. But then there's a load of people you're meant to mix with, most of them drinking alcohol. It's a strange experience, really – trying to do both things at once can be challenging. So with that first painting, it felt like a snapshot of a larger series. I think it can sometimes feel overwhelming at a private view, and I do detach a little bit and start looking at the people around me. And there are moments when you're not talking to someone and you're thinking, 'I should be talking to someone,' or 'What should I be doing now?' and you start focusing in on certain people. It's like a really intense version of people-watching, a speeded-up version of it.

CH: It's interesting that you talk about detachment, because there is clearly an element of that in these series of paintings. I was wondering how intentional that is.

BS: In the *Exclamations!* series I wasn't specifically thinking about that at the time, but once I'd painted them I realised there was a sense of dislocation, of people seeming distant. And so this was something I wanted to bring out more in the next series, *You and I*.

CH: The *Exclamations!* paintings have monochrome backgrounds, but the *You and I* series have very eclectic, arresting motifs, patterns and shapes behind the figures. Can you tell me about this?

BS: After the monochrome colour backgrounds to the *Exclamations!* paintings, I had the idea of painting really close-up details of large paintings on the walls behind the people at an exhibition. I thought this might capture something of the strangeness of a private view: there's a work in the background, there's a person in front of it, and then there's an event going on in that space around them as well. Perhaps the sense of detachment comes when you're switching from one mode of looking at an artwork to then thinking about having some kind of interaction with a person. And because the paintings are so small in scale, I was interested in the idea of creating a much larger sense of scale within the paintings – they're small paintings representing much larger paintings, in a much larger space.

CH: The figures you depict are full of character, almost inviting you to imagine their personalities.

BS: A lot of them have these public domain photos as starting points, but then drift off into their own reality. It does feel a bit like inventing a person in these paintings, which is very different to when I have made paintings of people I know; in that context it's about finding empathy and connection with the person, whereas in these paintings you're trying to conjure up this imagined life. It's like painting ghosts, in a way.

CH: So they're like amalgams. You have a starting point, but then they morph into the person as you're painting them, or the person comes into being as you're painting. How do you go about making the paintings?

BS: There's quite a particular way that I paint these paintings, which evolved through the *Exclamations!* series. I put down a brightly coloured ground – usually fluorescent pink to start with – and then a layer of white paint over that. Then that dries a little bit, and it gives you this slightly unstable surface that you can paint onto.

CH: And why do you do that?

BS: Partly just to have something that isn't the plain board to work against. But using the same colour background, when I was thinking about the series, brings a kind of colour coherence across the works. But also the fluorescent pink is quite an odd colour, and it's an unnatural colour, so it's particularly interesting to paint against. What I'll often do is, with a quite big brush, very quickly brush in the person and get some tones and a sense of the shape of the person's face, and then wipe it with a cloth, so a lot of it comes away. And so you're left with those pinks coming through and places where the paint's dried a bit more. You end up with a quite fragmented face. Then I'll tend to go in with a background colour to define the silhouette of the person a bit more. That's the process of getting to know this person in relation to the photograph that I'm working from. And then with the *You and I* series, I start getting a sense of what painting I might create behind them by trying to make some kind of visual connection with the character. Then I go in with a bit more detail and more layers, building up the portrait of the person. Normally there's a point where it becomes resolved in the character's eyes. When it feels like they're looking at me or looking at something, that's the point I tend to leave them.

CH: So there's like a moment of recognition, a realisation that a painting is finished?

BS: Definitely. And it can literally be the difference between a mark one way or the other, and then something falls into place. What's been good about doing the *You and I* series is that I feel like I'm a bit better at knowing when it's all slotted into place, even if some of them feel slightly unfinished. But once the eyes are working that usually feels like the time to stop. There's a point during the process where I stop looking at the photograph, where it's helped get the structure but then I'm ready to leave it behind. So then it's almost like switching into thinking about what will make this work as a painting.

CH: And what role does colour have in that construction of the character or the identity?

BS: A lot really. When I was about twelve, my mum decided that as I liked art, she would buy me this weekly magazine – *The Great Artists: Their lives, works and inspirations*. There are ninety-six of them. It's terrible, there are just two women artists in it, ninety-four male artists. It goes through the history of Western art, but from a very male perspective. There were a few issues that really stayed with me. The Matisse issue, for example, it's the green stripe on the nose there – that captured my imagination, just the effect of that green stripe and the colour. This comes through quite directly in the *Exclamations!* series, I think. I realised that because I'm painting from black and white photographs, as long as the paintings retain those tonal values, the colours can be whatever you want. Because I'm drawn to unnatural colours I enjoy working with those alien colours for people's faces.

CH: A lot of these characters look uncomfortable at this exhibition opening. Do you feel awkward yourself at these events?

BS: I don't know really. When I was younger, I used to get quite anxious about openings. They are always quite a strange experience and I would cope with the social anxiety I was feeling by drinking. An evening could take quite a wild shift over the space of two or three hours, where you go from feeling quite restrained to doing karaoke, belting out Eminem and dancing with strangers! How's that happened over this short period of time with these people? So I think I have quite mixed feelings.

CH: And presumably this awkwardness is even more keenly felt if it's your own exhibition opening?

BS: Yes! It's this weird pinnacle of so much work and effort that condenses down to two hours. And then there's quite often the inevitable slump afterwards. There's a lot of those elements and anxieties coming in, and I'm putting some of those onto the people I'm painting, while trying to understand something of them as well. Particularly when I was younger at openings, it would all feel a bit like a puzzle. How do I talk to this person, or what do I talk to this person about? And having these moments of being really conscious of hearing what I'm saying, a sort of inner critique that's running through your head: 'What are you talking about? This is ridiculous.' So it's a lot of those feelings coming through when I'm painting them, but much of the process is about trying to bring it to some kind of resolution or calmness by the time the painting's ended, and then there's traces of that left in these paintings. Maybe I can feel all of those things in the paintings. There are moments of awkwardness, moments of embarrassment, moments of joy, moments of connection, but all fleeting.

CH: I was thinking about that idea of being alone together. So many artists that I speak to feel exactly like you at that idea of performing an identity in a social context, like an art opening or in the wider art world. As creative people we get in this social soup together, and we're trying to figure out how to communicate or how to connect with each other. Within the *Exclamations!* series each painting has an alphabet-based exclamation for its title. How do you select those exclamations, and how are they connected to the image you've painted?

BS: With that first series it was a mixture of things I've overheard people saying. It gets difficult with some of the letters of the alphabet, like z and x...

CH: Why did you decide to use the alphabet?

BS: The very first painting was called *Exactly!*. In my mind, that was what I heard the person in the painting saying, but with an exclamation mark.

CH: I'm just looking through some of them. I love the titles!

BS: It was quite a fine balance. I was worried that it was tipping over into parody with some of the titles, a bit like the overexuberance that often comes across online. I had this idea that I could do one for each letter of the alphabet. So I had *Exactly!*, and then I could work through and make a different word that would sum up what I'd been thinking about while making each painting. It was quite easy when there were quite a few of the letters available, but then it did get harder, like for z: *Zounds!*. It's almost *Scooby-Doo*-ish, but it was trying to capture some kind of spirit of conversation, or that slightly heightened conversation that can happen in those circumstances where you're just having a chat. There's a sense you are using language you might not normally use. I find my accent or language will shift a bit while I'm having different conversations at an exhibition opening, or use different, self-conscious ways of speaking. I do worry that some of the titles might seem a bit damning!

CH: I love them! Some make me laugh out loud. *Tip Top!* made me chuckle.

BS: That's a real one I overheard.

CH: I like that. Some of them feel incongruous with what I'm looking at. Like *Forever!*, where the woman with the pink nose and red hair and striking green coat seems melancholy and forlorn, so this gap opens up between the title and the painting, and you enter that imaginary space of a conversation.

BS: That's a good example. I'd imagined someone else was saying *Forever!* and she was feeling slightly, not annoyed, but thinking that's a very large term to use for what they've just described. I was interested in the idea of such conversations taking place. Sometimes I imagine the exclamations as things the characters are directly saying, other times something they're responding to, or that they're hearing someone else say – those random snippets of background chatter that you get at a gathering.

CH: That fluorescent pink that you were talking about, you can see that shining through in the hair and the nose. I'm really struck by the different ways of connecting with us through all of these things, through the heightened colour, the stare, the placement of the person inside the frame. But also there's something that's almost 'so wrong that it's right' in each of the paintings – something that's slightly off in all of them, and yet somehow you make it work. One of my favourites is *Heavens!* because of the character that you've conjured, with the pale pinks and the orange coming through, and the green of the neck and then the bright orange. But even just that word – *Heavens!* – I can almost imagine who it is that's saying it. I feel like I might actually know that person, and I'm pretty sure it's a real person.

BS: I gave that painting to a friend, and they said, 'I like it, but why have you given me a picture of X?' And I said, 'It's not them,' and they're saying, 'But it is.' So that has happened with a few of them. There've been a few where I've looked at them and I've gone, 'I actually have painted this person without realising it,' so I've had to alter it, not wanting it to look too much like them. The original photograph didn't look like that, but they've drifted towards it. But I feel like I have face types, and I'll go, 'Okay, you're a Martin,' or a specific person, but of course there are certain facial traits that are quite common, as there are with aspects of personalities.

CH: It's interesting how you've conjured personality through the colour and the form, but also there's still space for us to project. With *Exclamations!* there's a process of participating with somebody – the idea that you're in dialogue with another person, or trying to figure them out. Could you talk a little bit about *You and I* and how that's different for you?

BS: *You and I* grew directly out of the *Exclamations!* series. It became more about the idea of the different layers of things happening in an exhibition opening, where there's the work, there's the space, there's the person in the space, and then there's that shared space of talking to each other. I was interested in how that carries through to the process of looking at the paintings. So there's that space between me painting the painting and you the viewer looking at it, and then there's me looking at this person, there's you looking at this person, and then there's the person depicted as both a possible 'you' and 'I'. That was where the title *You and I* came from, and then I realised they're both letters. So I could leave those letters out of this next series and just do twenty-four paintings. Which was a system for me to hang it on.

CH: What about the backgrounds in this series?

BS: I liked the idea of having someone standing in front of a large painting, so you just see a section of it. The paintings within the exhibition become backdrops to seeing these people (and give their names to my paintings). So it's almost like we're looking at snapshots from an opening – you're looking around and there are all these instant judgements you might be making in your head about who this person is, what they're thinking or why they're there. The idea of these being people at an opening in the *Exclamations!* series came while I was painting them, whereas it was the starting point for the *You and I* series and then just seeing where it went from there.

CH: Something I noticed that seems different in *You and I* is that in the *Exclamations!* series, it feels more like we're observing these people, and they are detached or distanced from us. But in the *You and I* series, sometimes it feels like the person is more curious about us. In *Xylophone*, for example, there's a tilt of the head, which might indicate there's some kind of interest in us as well.

BS: I'm glad that comes through. I was keen to broaden the selection of poses, looking for different head positions and different angles. I think this leads to a different dynamic.

CH: It feels like there's more of a relationship with the character in these ones. In *Exclamations!* I actually quite like the fact that some of the characters couldn't care less about us! Because sometimes when we observe or speak with people we get that vibe from them; they're not interested in us at all. We might well experience this at some exhibition openings, and certainly in other kinds of art and social spaces.

BS: I know what you mean. I also decided not to make their noses a different colour in this series, which I know doesn't sound like a fundamental decision, but I think it did shift the paintings quite a lot; it has quite an impact when you have a different colour nose.

CH: [Laughs] What role does humour have in these paintings, and in your wider practice?

BS: I think I use humour a lot as a defence mechanism, especially at openings. I like to think that I am humorous, but then I suppose we all do. I always wonder how much of the humour comes through. It always feels like the work's not too far from being a bit sad as well, and it's quite a fine balance between humour and melancholy. I think humour can offer a way into a work for people, and it can be a means of dealing with very serious stuff as well. Humour is one way of connecting with people and introducing them to what's going on. I think it's what Phil and I do in Juneau Projects and it carries over into the work I make on my own. I do create stupid videos as well and write poems that are a bit silly, and that's quite consciously foregrounding the humour. But it is always a bit of an icebreaker for me.

CH: It strikes me that it also affords you the opportunity to take more risks, pushing the edges of something; that pathos, empathy, melancholy that often comes up in your work. I don't know if you experienced this, but when I went to art college, portraiture was not something that was encouraged. It was almost a case of do anything *but* a still life or a portrait. So it's interesting to me that you're returning to portraiture in these two series.

BS: I had a very similar art college education in that there was a lot of talk about painting being dead. And there was a sense of artists reacting to the canon of art history and wanting to push forward. I remember installing an exhibition by the Swiss painter Jean-Frédéric Schnyder at Ikon many years ago. I was putting some of his paintings up and he was just having a wander around the gallery. He was maybe in his late fifies at this point and clearly in a very different stage of life to me as a twenty-two-year old, slightly hungover, trying to put some paintings up! He was really nice. He started chatting with me and asking, 'Do you make art?' We were talking a bit about that, and he just said to me at the end, 'You'll come back to painting one day. We all do.' And then just wandered off. At the time I thought, 'I will never come back to painting!' But he was right.

CS: There is a real playfulness in both series, but there is a certain pathos that comes out in the works when paying attention to a human and the minutiae of their appearances and traits.

BS: I was thinking about it a little while ago. I spent a lot of time on my own as a kid and that's why it used to feel so special going round to someone else's house. I remember my friend Royston had four older sisters and his mum and his dad, and his aunties would quite often be around as well. And you're just sitting in this living room and thinking, 'This is bonkers. There are ten people all doing stuff and it's loud and there's lots going on.' I really remember those moments watching his mum peel the potatoes for tea or that kind of thing, those little instants when you're thinking, 'We don't do tea like that,' and really loving those little things. Or being fascinated watching my girlfriend put her make-up on and thinking, 'This is incredible, what is going on here.' It's those little connections; they may seem quite trivial, but they're so powerful in terms of a feeling, resonance or connection. They are the little memories that play through my head almost like a really mundane YouTube. And then the sounds can be different as well.

CH: It's funny you should mention sound. What you're describing is like a processing of time in some way. There's a way of recalling not just the image, but the feeling that's inside at the same time as you see the thing. You write poems and you make music as well. And obviously those things have got a rhythm and a relationship to time in a different way. Does music or the rhythm of poetry inform your painting at all?

BS: I think so, definitely. While making the *You and I* series I was writing quite a lot of haikus. They are also quite mundane, a lot of them. You've got seventeen syllables to make a poem so it strips it down to 'what do you want to say?' You have to work it a lot. And sometimes they work, sometimes they don't. What is it you want to express in that short number of words? A little bit like writing a tweet. There's a concision, but it's the stuff that's unsaid as well. There are no words in the paintings, so how can you capture those said and unsaid things? I was getting towards finishing these paintings and I was listening to a song on the way back home from work one day. It was a song from the early 2000s that really took me back to a particular moment, a time and a place. I put it on repeat and then got home and made a painting of a mixtape. It's just a picture of a cassette, but there was some strange resonance in it – it really seemed to connect with people. It's my little taste of having gone viral on Instagram. It felt like putting the paint on the board, making this thing that looked like an old cassette, was somehow capturing this weird nostalgia for this time from my youth. If I knew how to do this every time that would be great! Painting can evoke all sorts of memories and feelings, however small.

CH: In relation to these feelings, what does painting give you that the other art forms don't?

BS: I do get distinct feelings from different ways of making. With music, I always feel like I don't really know what I'm doing, but I can reach a point where I have made something that I like the sound of, though I don't really know how I got there. With painting, I feel like there's an element of that, but I know that if I need to, I can make a piece that looks like a thing and I can work with that and play around with it. What I don't know is the moment when that resonance comes in. But the point when I stop with a painting is when it reaches this point of stillness. It's similar to when I try and meditate sometimes. It's quite hard – the cat will often leap on you while you're doing it! If you lie down or sit down on the floor, he always wants to get involved! But there is that point where it's about just being in the moment. Because a lot of the time you're flitting between thoughts of things that have happened, things that are happening or are going to happen; there's always those preoccupations. And the moment of completion does not have any of that, for me. I think that's one of the beautiful things about making – that moment of stillness. You're just there in the world and the world's there.

CH: One thing that I have always loved about you and your work, and particularly in these paintings, is being able to be super present. It's like you've got this perfect balance of being able to say what needs to be said and to be present in this way, but also it's not too much, it's just enough. There's something warm and deliciously cheeky in some of the paintings, and then there are others where that sadness or that feeling of being alone is more tangible. It's quite an amazing thing to have that ability to move between those registers in your work.

BS: Thank you, that's more than I could hope for from the paintings! It does always feel like peaks and troughs. I think it happens for a lot of people with painting. It is an emotional rollercoaster: 'This is great, this is the worst painting ever, it's great again, I've just ruined it.' It's torture in some ways; a really nice torture! And when it works, when it has that resolution, it's the end of a beautiful journey.

CH: Something that just came to me, maybe because we were talking about music: it's like the combination that you find in the Bee Gees and the Beach Boys, maybe. They are both incredibly weird. It's so weird, but somehow reaches a harmonious state.

BS: The Beach Boys are insane. There's a song of theirs, 'The Warmth of the Sun', that has always really stuck with me. I used it in a sculpture I made when I was in my early twenties. But it's exactly that. It's the most beautiful song and it's heartbreaking and joyous and just so weird because they're all singing in falsetto voices doing these strange whoops and it shouldn't work. But it's just phenomenal.

CH: That's a nice place to end. Thank you for sharing about your paintings. It's been such a treat and I'm such a fan. I could live with all of them quite happily!

Ben Sadler was born in Birmingham (UK) in 1977. He was an only child and spent a lot of time drawing and hanging out with the family cats. His teenage years were spent obsessing over music, books and art before attending the Ruskin School of Fine Art, Oxford (1995–98), and the Royal College of Art, London (2002–04). Since 2001 he has been one half of the artist duo Juneau Projects with his friend Philip Duckworth, while also making his own paintings, music, poems, and videos. He lives in Birmingham with Katy, Hazel and their cat Oscar.

Deborah Kermode is the CEO and Artistic Director of Midlands Arts Centre (MAC) and has been in her role since 2016. Before that she was Deputy Director at Ikon Gallery in Birmingham, and she has also worked as Director of Bright Space, an arts education charity for children and young people.

Catherine O'Flynn is a novelist whose writing has received various awards including a British Book Award and the Costa First Novel Award. Fay Weldon described O'Flynn as 'the JG Ballard of Birmingham… finding poetry and meaning where others see merely boredom and dereliction'.

Ceri Hand is a creative coach, host of the *Extraordinary Creatives* podcast, and founder of cerihand.com, where she offers coaching, workshops, courses, masterminds and a membership community for contemporary artists. Dedicated to helping creatives overcome fears, make impactful work and boost their earnings, Ceri draws on over thirty years in the arts as an artist, curator and director of renowned galleries and institutions. Her experience spans every facet of the creative world – from leading art magazines and festivals to overseeing residency programmes. She is also Co-Chair of Castlefield Gallery, Manchester.

Ben Sadler
You and I

Published by Hurtwood Press Limited, London
Part of the Hurtwood Contemporary Artist Series
Commissioning editor: Matt Price
Series design: Agatha Smith

The Hurtwood Contemporary Artist Series aims to spotlight a talented and diverse range of artists whether established or early in their careers. Each publication showcases a significant body of work or exhibition by a single artist with high-quality reproductions and features a foreword and an essay by leading writers and curators. Dynamic and forward looking, Hurtwood's Contemporary Artist Series responds to culture as it happens, documenting the work of artists working nationally and internationally today.

Artist acknowledgements: Many thanks to my friend Matt Price for his vision and support; to Deborah Kermode, Ceri Hand and Catherine O'Flynn for their inspiration and wisdom; to Eelke Jan Bles, Samantha Schneider, Marg Watkinson, Simon Willis, Oliver Jones, Sarah Waldron, Shaun Morris, and Adriaan Van Hoorn and Gertie Geradts for their support of the *Exclamations!* series; to David Rowan for his excellent photography; to Stuart and Katy Acquaye-Tonge for their enduring friendship; to Phil Duckworth for putting up with my whistling; to my mom Hazel for never not believing that I would like painting one day; to my dad Mike and my stepmom Sue for that first oil paint set; to Hazel and Oscar for making each day a pleasure; and to Katy for both her unwavering love and continued overlooking of all the paint stains on the sofa and carpet.

Project editor: Matt Price
Proofreading: William Lambie
Layout design: Jenny Kohler
Reprography and production: Hurtwood Press

Texts © Deborah Kermode, Catherine O'Flynn and Ceri Hand
Work © Ben Sadler
Photography © David Rowan

Published in 2025 by Hurtwood Press Limited, London
© Hurtwood Press Limited, London

ISBN 978-0-903696-96-8

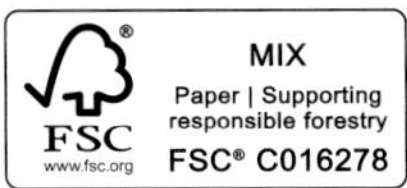

Printed and bound in the UK by Halstan using FSC® Mix

Cover image: *Apple* (detail), 2024

Published in association with:

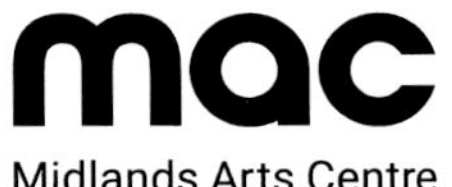

Midlands Arts Centre